Southern Living WITHDRAWN

COTTAGES & RETREATS *Style*

MORE THAN 130 OF OUR FAVORITE HOME PLANS

Published by Hanley Wood
One Thomas Circle, NW, Suite 600
Washington, DC 20005

General Manager, Plans Services, David Rook
Associate Publisher, Development, Jennifer Pearce
Manager, Customer Service, Michael Morgan
Director, Marketing, Mark Wilkin

Editor, Simon Hyoun
Publications Manager, Brian Haefs
Production Manager, Theresa Emerson
Manager, Plans & Web Operations, Geoffrey Taft
Plan Merchandiser, Hillary Gottemoeller
Graphic Artist, Joong Min
Director, Audience Development, Erik Schulze

Hanley Wood Corporate
Chief Executive Officer, Frank Anton
Chief Financial Officer, Matthew Flynn
Chief Administrative Officer, Frederick Moses
Chief Information Officer, Jeffrey Craig
Executive Vice President/Corporate Sales, Ken Beach
Vice President/Finance, Brad Lough
Vice President/Legal, Mike Bender
Interim Vice President/Human Resources, Bill McGrath
Controller, Virginia Jackson

Most Hanley Wood titles are available at quantity discounts with
bulk purchases for educational, business, or sales promotional use.
For information, please contact Mark Wilkin at mwilkin@hanleywood.com.

VC Graphics
Creative Director, Veronica Vannoy
Graphic Designer, Jennifer Gerstein
Graphic Designer, Denise Reiffenstein
Graphic Designer, Jeanne-Erin Worster

Photo Credits
Front Cover (top) and pp. 6–7: Design HPK3400119 by ©Southern Living
Front Cover (bottom left and center), Back Cover (top left, top center and bottom) and pp. 28–33:
Design HPK3400011 by ©*Coastal Living*/Brian Vanden Brink
Front Cover (bottom right), and p. 104: Design HPK3400025 by ©Southern Living
Back Cover (top right), and pp. 162–163: Design HPK3400085 by ©Southern Living

Design
Cover and Book Design, Deana Callison for Southern Living

Distribution Center
PBD
Hanley Wood Consumer Group
3280 Summit Ridge Parkway
Duluth, Georgia 30096

10 9 8 7 6 5 4 3 2 1

Printed in the United States of America

Library of Congress Control Number: 2008923457

ISBN-13: 978-1-931131-76-6
ISBN-10: 1-931131-76-7

COTTAGES & RETREATS

Lakeside Cottage, page 24

West Bay Landing, page 12

4 INTRODUCTION

There's a lot to love in the perfect cottage retreat. Every home collected here offers loads of personal comfort, seasonal living, and great entertaining.

6 FEATURE HOMES

See for yourself the skilled craft behind each of these fine home designs.

34 LESS THAN 1,500 SQ. FT.

In a variety of styles, these homes are ideal for small families and vacationers.

59 1,500–2,000 SQ. FT.

Find increased flexibility in these slightly larger family designs.

96 2,000–2,500 SQ. FT.

Dedicated spaces for dining and work may make these plans right for you.

140 OVER 2,500 SQ. FT.

Formal separation of rooms and more privacy for homeowners are found in these homes.

162 GAZEBOS AND GARDEN STRUCTURES

The perfect finish to any landscape plan.

170 HOW TO ORDER

What's included in a plans package and a full list of prices.

Southern Living® Style

MORE THAN 130 OF OUR FAVORITE HOMES

THE PERFECT COTTAGE RETREAT

Comfortable, carefree,

and cooled by passing breezes—every home in this book promises a skillful balance of spaces for entertaining, private enjoyment, and rejuvenation. If you're looking to build a vacation home on the water, a mountain cabin, or just a primary residence for your family, this collection of under–3,000 square foot homes and cottages has the designs you've been searching for.

Though no single architectural style defines today's cottage, the homes still favor small footprints, natural materials, simple construction, and coordinated indoor-outdoor spaces. For their size and spirit of seasonal living, cottages are often ideal for the waterfront.

Below: West Bay Landing's (page 12) summer camp design contains practical working spaces like this home office.

Below Right: Nautical Cottage (page 6) shows how family living is a key part of cottage life.

©SOUTHERN LIVING

©SOUTHERN LIVING

©COASTAL LIVING EMILY MINTON-REDFIELD

Because interaction with the outdoors is such an essential part of enjoying cottage life, we've included a section of garden and project plans in the back of the book. The section contains gazebos, sheds, playhouses, and other structures that complement the architectural style and design of the homes. Choose the home and a project plans together, either to be built at once or separately. Depending on the project plan and your local codes, a building permit may or may not be required—do-it-yourselfers, take note.

Food tastes better and company stays longer in the right environment—your next home home can be an elegant, easy-living plan, with appreciation for modest comforts. Find it inside. ❀

Above: The Bermuda Bluff (page 8) has the kind of warm welcome people love in a cottage.
Below: Bedrooms are designed for comfort and privacy, such as this master suite from Our Gulf Coast Cottage (page 26).

©SOUTHERN LIVING

Nautical Cottage

Cottage, with Style

South Carolina inspired
and full of charm

A perfectly charming

home designed by Scott Ziegler of Ziegler Cooper Architects, the Nautical Cottage packs abundant indoor and outdoor living spaces into its modest footprint. An extensive wraparound covered porch reaches around three sides of the home for enjoyment of lakeside views. On one side of the home, the porch is enclosed by a screen so that home owners and their guests may enjoy the outdoors without worrying about insects and inclement weather. A detailed porch railing lined with columns lends the exterior a simple elegance, while the variably pitched roofline combines with a dormer for additional architectural interest.

The entry is a single French door that leads into the combination kitchen and dining area. Double doors lead from this room to the screened porch, as well. Windows placed over the kitchen's main food prep stations provide an excellent vantage point to enjoy the views outside or to monitor children at play.

Nestled on the other side of the dining area is the cozy family room, made more spacious by the vaulted ceiling. Windows to the screened porch and to the back of the lot provide multiple vantage points.

Two bedrooms flank the hallway that extends from the kitchen. The hall also leads to the first floor's convenient full bath and washer/dryer area. The master bedroom conveniently sits atop the stairway that leads from the family room. An upstairs walk-in closet and multiple storage areas complete the layout of this thoughtfully designed lakeside cottage. ❈

For detailed information and floor plans, turn to page 54.

Opposite: Board siding and a neutral color create a timeless look for the covered porch.

Left: Throughout the home, simple wooden mantles, stained doors and windows complement the home's casual tone.

Below: Expressive rooflines and porch railing capture the home's playful spirit.

BERMUDA BLUFF

Low Country Elegance

Casual open living
spaces for families

Extended roof lines

and a centrally placed shed dormer emphasize the
Low Country simplicity of the Bermuda Bluff, designed
by Allison-Ramsey Architects. Inside, well-integrated
outdoor living areas and high ceilings create an open,
lofty feel. A screened porch and a patio are adjacent to
the family room, creating a spacious zone for casual
entertaining. Similarly, the kitchen works closely with
the family room, so the chef can entertain guests and
work at the same time.

Opposite: Beadboard walls and open,
sunlit spaces bring a waterfront flavor to the home.

Below: A well-proportioned fireplace anchors
the family room's conversation area.

BERMUDA BLUFF

With direct access to the patio, the master suite enjoys a private connection to the outdoors. The master bath is surprisingly luxurious for a home this size, with dual sinks, a spa tub, and separate shower. Note the placement of the His and Hers walk-in closets, separating the bath and ensuring peace between early risers and late sleepers.

A guest room is located in the upper-floor loft. Complete with a private bath, this comfortably sized retreat is perfect for kids or a couple visiting for the weekend. A third bedroom can be created at the front of the plan, attended as well by a full bath. Otherwise, use the space to wrap up light office work or as a reading room. ❀

For detailed information and floor plans, turn to page 95.

Left: The classic red metal roof is punctuated by a large shed dormer.

Below Left: A center island adds prep space and storage to the efficient kitchen.

Below: The screen porch is deep enough to work as an entertaining space.

WEST BAY LANDING

Southern Getaway

A home that blends resort-style
luxury with relaxed rusticity

This unique Southern

house plan combines all the warmth and welcome of a lodge with high-end amenities any family would appreciate. The Arts and Crafts style exterior blends indigenous materials with earth tones, creating a rugged look that is very much at home in the great outdoors.

The main entry leads directly into the mudroom. Screened open areas between horizontal slats create an ideal transition into the home's central living spaces, while keeping out bugs. Vacationers may store their outdoor gear and muddy boots in the mudroom's built-in cabinets and shelving to minimize clutter. The walkway past the mudroom leads directly to a screened porch for those who are not ready to head indoors.

Opposite: The exterior shows contemporary "camp" elements.

Left: A wall-mounted faucet and pail sink further emphasize the home's rustic aesthetic.

Above: Exposing the roof rafters created the summer-cabin feel the homeowners desired.

Top: Built-in storage and media cabinets control clutter in the family room.

WEST BAY LANDING

The central hall serves as the spine of the home, with the formal dining room, kitchen, and master suite branching off on one side. The dining room's proximity to other open spaces allows for abundant natural lighting. Open entries to a family room, an office space, and the kitchen enhance the room's spaciousness.

The master bedroom on the main level provides private access to enclosed relaxation on the screened porch via a set of double doors. The master bathroom, which can also be accessed from the kitchen area, offers dual sinks that flank the window in the master bath.

Stairs lead up from the kitchen to a hallway that runs the length of the home. The hall is lined with additional built-in storage for decorative displays or easy access to toys and games—making the hall an instant playroom.

Below: Great light in a home feels open and spacious.

At one end of the hall lies the guestroom, where a low-slung, built-in window seat fills the space neatly between two enclosed spaces that can serve either as closets or locations for additional shelving or storage.

The children's room at the opposite end of the hallway is large enough to sleep several kids while placing them at a discrete distance from both guests and the master suite.

The outdoor kitchen, just past a set of wooden double doors, contains all the utility of the main kitchen indoors, with the added benefit of a grill that's perfect for family cookouts. A long built-in table ensures that homeowners and their guests can enjoy outdoor dining. ❁

For detailed information and floor plans, turn to page 101.

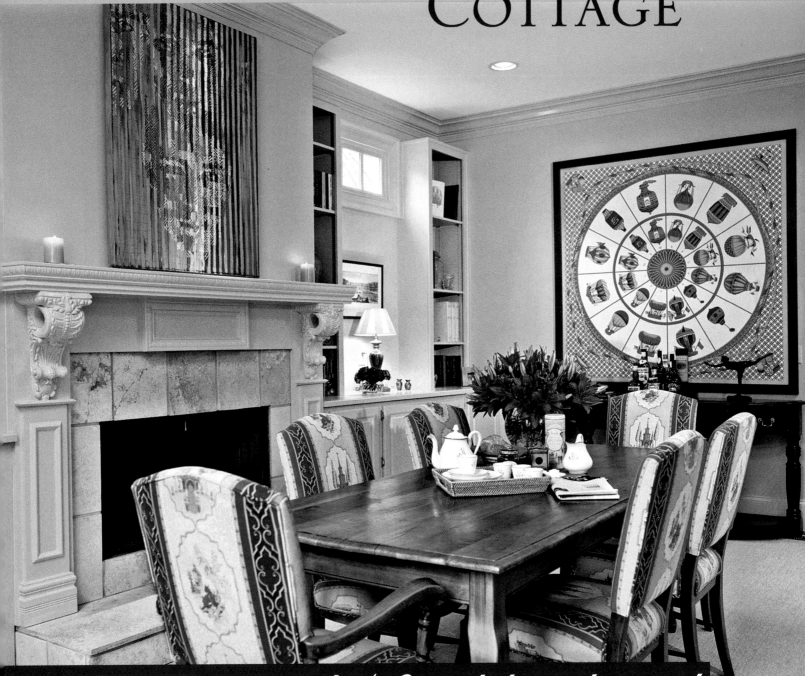

RIVER VIEW
COTTAGE

Traditional Neighborhood

A family home balancing
formal and casual spaces

Reminiscent of

the Greek Revival houses of historic Southern waterfront towns like Savannah, the River View Cottage by Looney Ricks Kiss Architects shows the polish of classic form with the charm of modest, cottage-style living. The result is a design with timeless appeal and an intuitive floor plan in which formality and function work together.

This compact plan provides transitional elements between living zones. For instance, the well-proportioned covered porch and small foyer at the front of the plan help bring visitors into the fold of intimate interior spaces such as the dining room and family room. Likewise, the sunroom acts as a buffer zone between the living spaces and rear-loading garage.

Opposite: A substantial hearth elevates the formal tone of the dining room.

Below: By contrast, the eat-in kitchen is casual and familiar.

RIVER VIEW COTTAGE

Above: The size and scope of this landscape plan feels just right for the 2,300-square-foot home.
Right: Two identical archways separate the dining room and living room.
Opposite: The curbside elevation is strictly traditional, noting fine columns and French doors.

Traditional placement of the bedrooms on the second floor means more square footage for the family room and kitchen on the main level. Privacy between bedrooms is also maximized by strategically placed closets and baths. Notice the location of the laundry area—smartly situated within easy reach of all members of the family and close to where laundry "occurs."

The master suite is especially comfortable, featuring a private covered porch and fireplace. A double-bowl vanity and separate tub and shower make sharing this space easy. ✸

For detailed information and floor plans, turn to page 121.

2007 Cottage Living
Idea Home

A Winning Combination

Two-story living and
loads of style

When building on

a lot that offers far greater depth than width, one doesn't need to compromise on room space, amenities, or any other elements that make a house a home. Designed by Eric Moser, Moser Design Group, the 2007 Cottage Living Idea Home proves just that, artfully bringing together classic Southern details with an economical design. The result: a house plan that is tailor-made for those who don't want to sacrifice the luxuries of home despite limited space on their lot.

A classic front porch with a second-level balcony overhead—both of which are neatly lined with columns—presents those who approach with a warm welcome. The enclosed parking area to the left side of the house plan easily doubles as a garden or courtyard for an outdoor private retreat. A covered porch in back with plenty of room for multiple chairs completes the outdoor living spaces.

Opposite: Reminiscent of the Charleston Single House style, this design is ideal for narrow lots.

Above: Interior spaces are airy and open, making the most of the nine-foot ceilings.

2007 Cottage Living
Idea Home

Just inside the front entry, a parlor room boasts built-in shelving and window-seats, setting the mood of relaxation right from the start. A hallway leads from the parlor to the parking enclosure, a simple powder room, and the rooms in the back of the plan.

At the end of the hall, a kitchen that fills the width of the plan provides chefs with two L-shaped countertops as well as a central island with a built-in sink. Past the kitchen, a generously proportioned living room is large enough to offer space for dining, as well. A series of three French doors open from the dining/living room combo to the back porch, while a fireplace warms the room in chillier weather.

From the kitchen, a winding stairway leads up to all three bedrooms. An enormous walk-in closet serves the master bedroom from the central hallway. The master bedroom's bath boasts an oversized tub, as well as twin vanities—as does the central bathroom that serves the other two bedrooms on this level. The master bedroom also includes private access via two French doors to the balcony that extends over the front porch—the perfect vantage point from which to greet houseguests. ❀

For detailed information and floor plans, turn to page 127.

Opposite: Stainless steel appliances and crisp, white cabinetry brighten the kitchen.

Above: Doubling as a formal living room, the parlour acts as a semi-formal entry space and entertaining area.

Left: Located on the second floor, the master bedroom features a private porch.

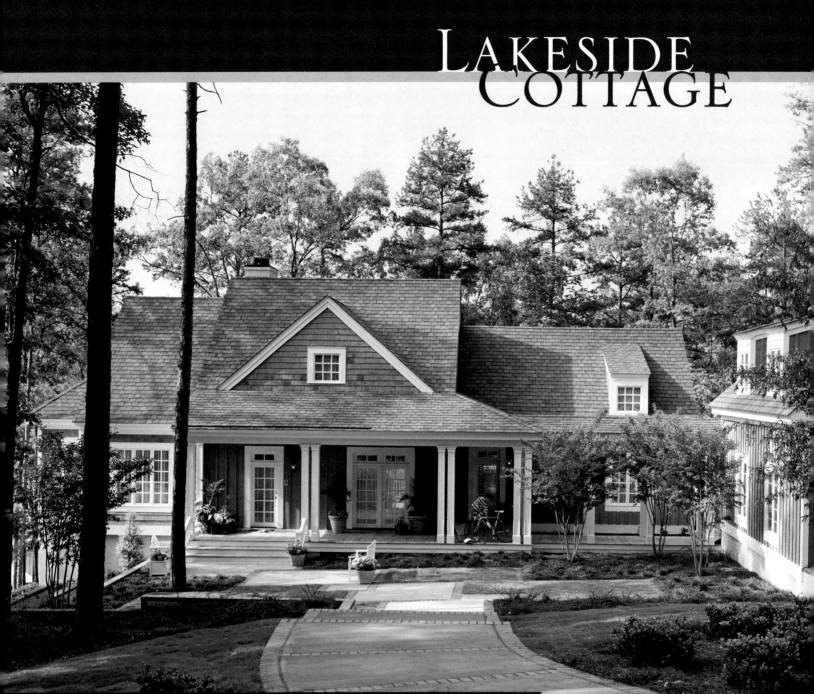

LAKESIDE COTTAGE

Waterfront Appeal

A perfectly planned family-sized
home with great amenities

Opposite Above: The wide front porch leads into a covered walkway between the main house and garage.

Opposite Below: The casually defined dining room reaches the porch at two points, via French doors.

Left and Below: Dining and gathering areas are found at both ends of the home.

This plan

designed by William Phillips seems tailor made for the growing family looking for a home with practical amenities. The kitchen-side entry leads quickly from the garage—a nice accommodation when carrying groceries. The brief utility space just inside the door serves as a mudroom, providing a sink and laundry area, as well as counters and storage for family members leaving for the day or coming home.

Other niceties include the large bath shared between the smaller bedrooms at the left of the plan. Pocket doors and a single-bowl vanity has allowed room for the inclusion of a corner shower and full-sized tub. Windows surround the bath, for light and ventilation. The bedrooms themselves are equally well daylit; one even has direct access to the rear foyer and deck.

The design features great outdoor living spaces at the back of the plan. The covered porch just inside from the deck provides for casual dining and entertaining occasions, highlighting views of the back of the property. The space also functions to control the amount of natural light entering the living room on hot summer days.

Finally, the relationship between the master suite and kitchen helps homeowners find the time for a quick meal before work. Inside the suite, a small fireplace and built-in media center bring a touch of luxury to the home. Deep walk-in closets and well-defined bath areas also bring a sense of ease and comfort to the suite. ❀

For detailed information and floor plans, turn to page 140.

OUR GULF COAST
COTTAGE

Coastal Charm

Simply designed
and easy to enjoy

This masterful

floor plan by William Phillips shows that a cleverly designed one-level home can offer just as much variety and living space options as a larger home.

Raised high on brick piers to keep its owners cool and dry, this cottage calls to mind the traditional Lowcountry homes of the South. The square, gently sloping hipped roof covers the porch that wraps around three sides of the home. The broad, deep gallery forms a functional porch detailed by in-laid columns.

Just past the double doors of the centered entryway, a foyer is symmetrically flanked by the living room on one side and the dining room on the other. Additional double doors lead from both of these rooms to the porch. The hallway ends at the family room. A pair of French doors lead from the family room to a courtyard in back, with garden pool.

Throughout the home, wide cased openings create one spacious sweep of space, while the perimeter gallery affords spillover space for parties. Ceiling heights are 10 feet throughout the house. The working plans for the cottage include a separate double garage with a similar look. ❁

For detailed information and floor plans, turn to page 139.

Opposite: Found at the front of the plan, the formal dining room has surrounding views of the property.

Below Left: Designed for warm weather, the home accesses the porch at multiple points.

Below: The spacious living room separates the master suite from the rest of the home.

COTTAGE
OF THE YEAR

A Cottage of Details

Traditional good looks
and innovative planning

On the outside,

a front-facing gable and a classic porch that spans the width of the plan gives Cottage of the Year—designed by Eric Moser of Moser Design Group—streetside presence. With its simple porch details, the home is suitable for any traditional neighborhood. But a closer look at this design reveals an organized, comfortable home designed for entertaining, casual enjoyment, and everyday living.

Start with the combined space at the center of that plan that brings together the family room, dining room, and kitchen into a single, flexible zone for family interaction. The open layout allows owners to move intuitively from the kitchen's cooking area to the dining area to the conversation area in front of the large fireplace. Large windows nearly surround this space, allowing in daylight and a sense of connection with the changing seasons. The screened porch just outside the kitchen, complete with a fireplace, adds yet another option for family time.

Overnight guests or live-in extended family will appreciate the private accommodation at the back of the plan. The guest cottage is a two-story apartment with full bath, walk-in closet, and porch. Furnish the lower level as a living room and the upstairs loft as a bedroom.

Likewise, the master suite is located in its own wing at the right of the plan. Similar to the guest cottage, the suite features a private porch, generous closets, and delightful bath with a gardenside tub. The shower is large enough to accommodate two bathers with ease. The sunny vestibule that leads to the suite will give the homeowners the feeling of being in their own retreat.

Upstairs bedrooms contain plenty of storage space with one walk-in and two reach-in closets. Separate vanities and a full tub make sharing easy. ❀

For detailed information and floor plans, turn to page 140.

Opposite: Great curb appeal suits the home well for corner lots.

Below: Built-in organization and decorative millwork bring a custom touch to every space.

COTTAGE
OF THE YEAR

Below: Floor-to-ceiling windows invite light into the home.

Right: Traditional design elements will suit the home well for any type of neighborhood.

Opposite: The master bath's standing tub provides a spa-like experience.

Opposite: Just outside the guest cottage, the screened porch is a well-placed seasonal space.

Above: There's plenty of counter space in the hard-working kitchen.

Left: The neighborhood-friendly design offers four-sided appeal.

Oak Creek

PLAN #HPK3400031

Designed by William H. Phillips

Square Footage: 412

Width: 20' - 0"

Depth: 36' - 0"

Foundation: Crawlspace

1-800-850-1491
eplans.com

1 *Bedroom* | 1 *Full Bath*

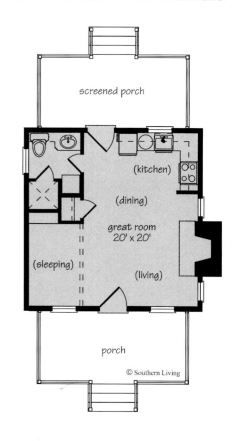

screened porch

(kitchen)

(dining)

great room
20' x 20'

(sleeping)

(living)

porch

© Southern Living

Beachside Bungalow

MUIR STEWART '05

| 1 *Bedroom* | 1 *Full Bath* |

PLAN #HPK3400041

Designed by Moser Design Group
for Coastal Living Magazine

Square Footage: 484

Width: 22' - 8"

Depth: 21' - 4"

Foundation: Crawlspace

1-800-850-1491
eplans.com

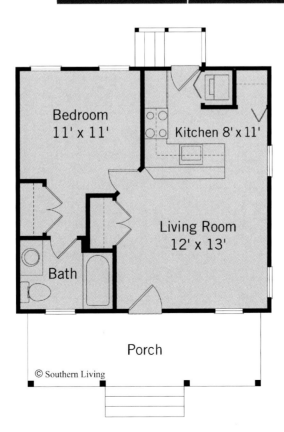

Bedroom
11' x 11'

Kitchen 8' x 11'

Living Room
12' x 13'

Bath

Porch

© Southern Living

Hilltop

PLAN #HPK3400012

Designed by William H. Phillips

Square Footage: 539

Width: 28' - 6"

Depth: 31' - 0"

Foundation: Crawlspace

1-800-850-1491
eplans.com

1 *Bedroom* | 1 *Full Bath*

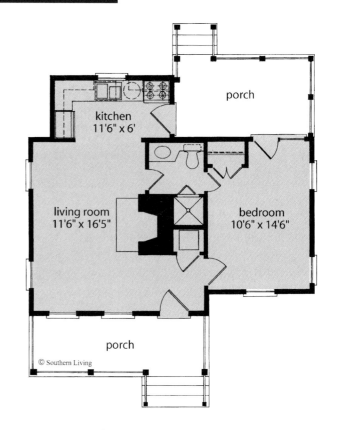

porch

kitchen
11'6" x 6'

living room
11'6" x 16'5"

bedroom
10'6" x 14'6"

porch

© Southern Living

Crooked Creek

1 *Bedroom* | 1 *Full Bath* | 1 *Half Bath*

PLAN #HPK3400033

Designed by William H. Phillips

First Floor: 409 sq. ft.

Second Floor: 222 sq. ft.

Total: 631 sq. ft.

Width: 24' - 8"

Depth: 25' - 4"

Foundation: Crawlspace

1-800-850-1491
eplans.com

First Floor

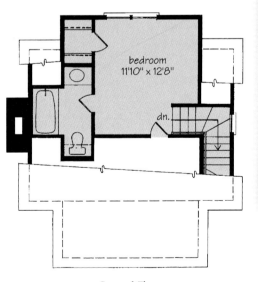

Second Floor

Eagle's Nest

PLAN #HPK3400032

Designed by William H. Phillips

First Floor: 384 sq. ft.

Second Floor: 250 sq. ft.

Total: 634 sq. ft.

Width: 24' - 0"

Depth: 29' - 0"

Foundation: Crawlspace

1-800-850-1491
eplans.com

| 1 *Bedroom* | 1 *Full Bath* | 1 *Half Bath* |

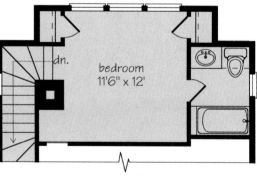

Second Floor

bedroom
11'6" x 12'
dn.

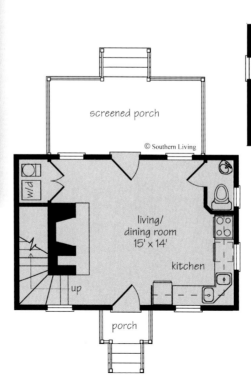

screened porch

© Southern Living

living/
dining room
15' x 14'

kitchen

w/d

up

porch

First Floor

ARCHITECTURAL RENDERING: ROLAND DAVIS

| 1 Bedroom | 2 Full Baths |

PLAN #HPK3400027

Designed by William H. Phillips

First Floor: 448 sq. ft.

Second Floor: 192 sq. ft.

Total: 640 sq. ft.

Width: 24' - 0"

Depth: 28' - 0"

Foundation: Crawlspace

1-800-850-1491
eplans.com

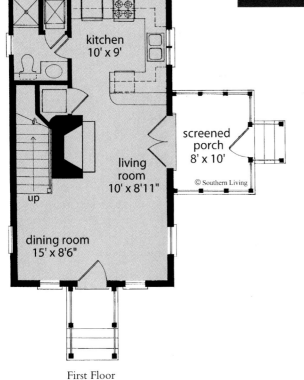

kitchen
10' x 9'

screened
porch
8' x 10'

© Southern Living

living
room
10' x 8'11"

up

dining room
15' x 8'6"

bedroom loft
12' x 10'

dn.

open to below

First Floor

Second Floor

Little Red

ARCHITECTURAL RENDERING: ROLAND DAVIS

PLAN #HPK3400014

Designed by William H. Phillips

First Floor: 562 sq. ft.

Second Floor: 238 sq. ft.

Total: 800 sq. ft.

Width: 22' - 6"

Depth: 33' - 0"

Foundation: Crawlspace

1-800-850-1491
eplans.com

1 *Bedroom* | 1 *Full Bath*

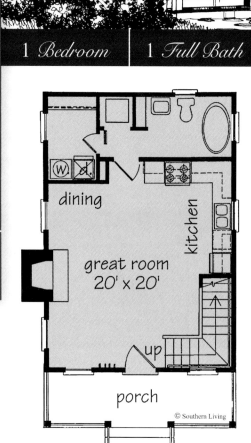

dining

kitchen

great room
20' x 20'

up

porch

© Southern Living

First Floor

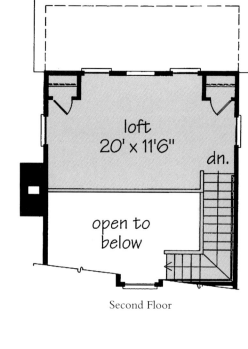

loft
20' x 11'6"

dn.

open to
below

Second Floor

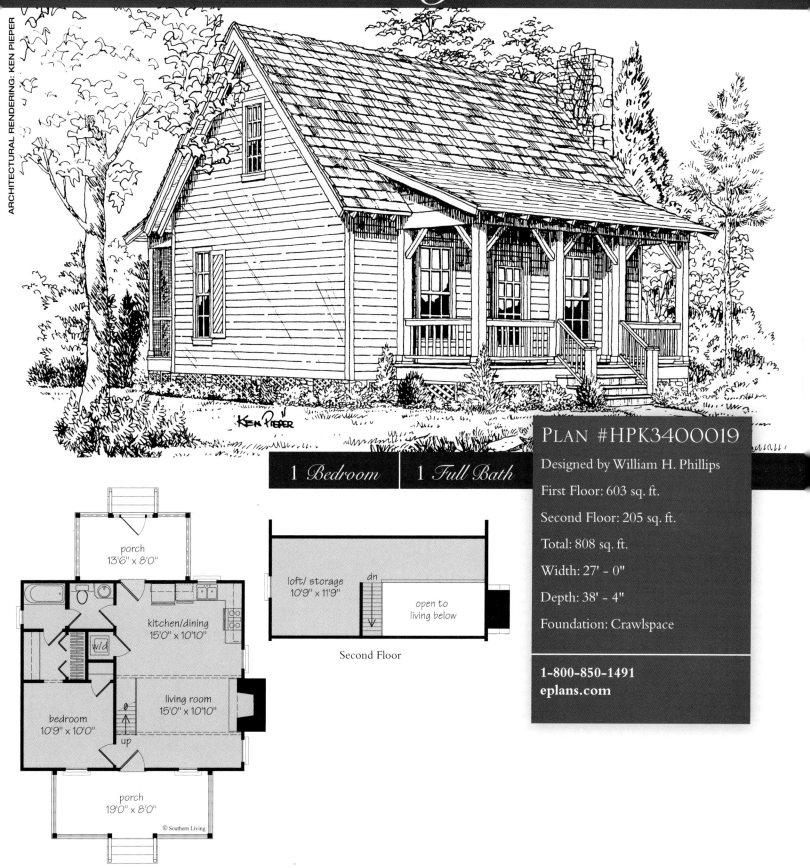

Grayson Trail

808 square feet

ARCHITECTURAL RENDERING: KEN PIEPER

1 *Bedroom* | **1** *Full Bath*

PLAN #HPK3400019

Designed by William H. Phillips

First Floor: 603 sq. ft.

Second Floor: 205 sq. ft.

Total: 808 sq. ft.

Width: 27' - 0"

Depth: 38' - 4"

Foundation: Crawlspace

1-800-850-1491
eplans.com

porch
13'6" x 8'0"

kitchen/dining
15'0" x 10'10"

w/d

bedroom
10'9" x 10'0"

living room
15'0" x 10'10"

up

porch
19'0" x 8'0"

© Southern Living

First Floor

loft/ storage
10'9" x 11'9"

dn

open to
living below

Second Floor

Mill Springs

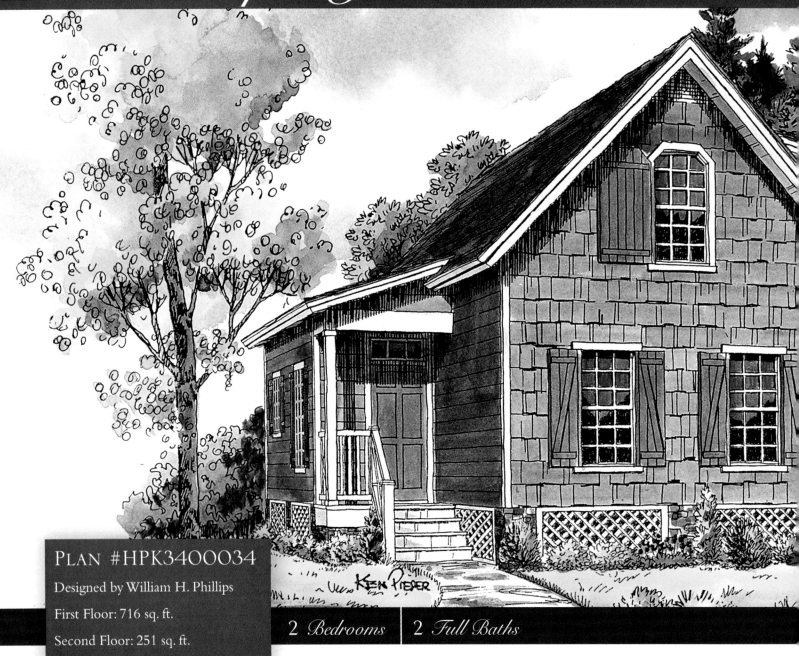

PLAN #HPK3400034

Designed by William H. Phillips

First Floor: 716 sq. ft.

Second Floor: 251 sq. ft.

Total: 967 sq. ft.

Width: 28' - 0"

Depth: 38' - 6"

Foundation: Crawlspace

1-800-850-1491
eplans.com

2 *Bedrooms* | 2 *Full Baths*

IDEAL FOR A SHORT GETAWAY or as a sportsman's cabin, yet comfortable enough for extended stays, Mill Springs is a perfect vacation residence. Materials such as stone, wood siding, and shingles bring out the home's natural character, while nine- and eight-foot ceilings establish a relaxing yet personal sense of scale. A more private second bedroom and bath are located upstairs. Completing the design is an optional water wheel, included in the blueprints. ❀

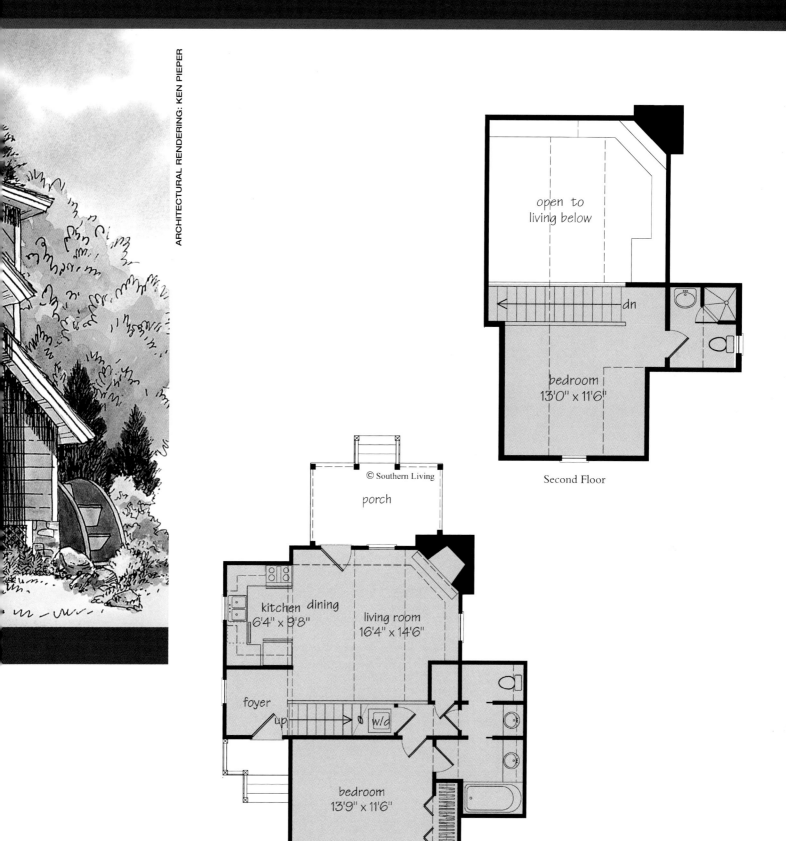

open to
living below

dn

bedroom
13'0" x 11'6"

Second Floor

© Southern Living

porch

kitchen dining
6'4" x 9'8"

living room
16'4" x 14'6"

foyer

up

w/d

bedroom
13'9" x 11'6"

First Floor

Deer Run

ARCHITECTURAL RENDERING: ROLAND DAVIS

PLAN #HPK3400013

Designed by William H. Phillips

First Floor: 763 sq. ft.

Second Floor: 210 sq. ft.

Total: 973 sq. ft.

Width: 28' - 0"

Depth: 36' - 0"

Foundation: Crawlspace

1-800-850-1491
eplans.com

2 Bedrooms | 2 Full Baths

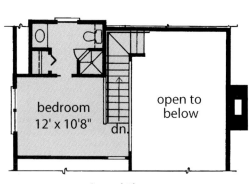

Second Floor

bedroom
12' x 10'8"

open to below

dn.

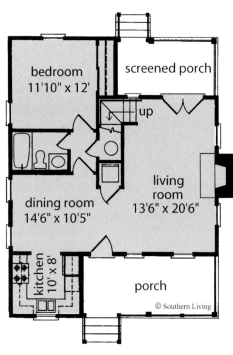

bedroom
11'10" x 12'

screened porch

up

living room
13'6" x 20'6"

dining room
14'6" x 10'5"

kitchen
10' x 8'

porch

© Southern Living

First Floor

The Ozarks

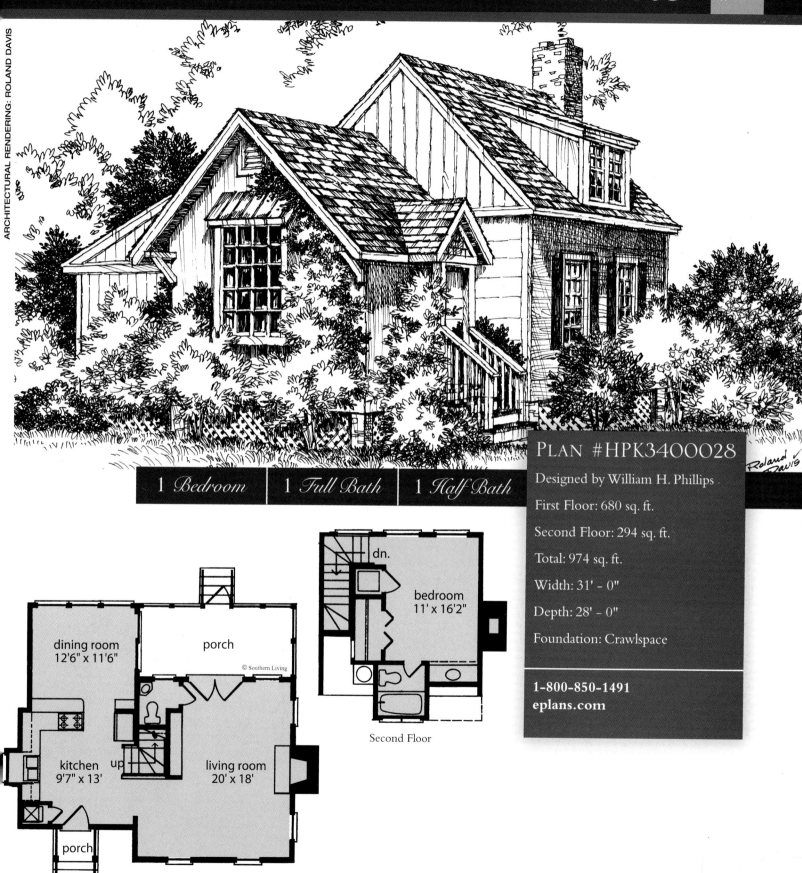

1 *Bedroom* | 1 *Full Bath* | 1 *Half Bath*

© Southern Living

PLAN #HPK3400028

Designed by William H. Phillips

First Floor: 680 sq. ft.

Second Floor: 294 sq. ft.

Total: 974 sq. ft.

Width: 31' - 0"

Depth: 28' - 0"

Foundation: Crawlspace

1-800-850-1491
eplans.com

dining room
12'6" x 11'6"

porch

kitchen
9'7" x 13'

up

living room
20' x 18'

porch

First Floor

dn.

bedroom
11' x 16'2"

Second Floor

Walnut Cove

ARCHITECTURAL RENDERING: KEN PIEPER

PLAN #HPK3400017

Designed by William H. Phillips

Square Footage: 1,086

Width: 34' – 0"

Depth: 51' – 2"

Foundation: Crawlspace

1-800-850-1491
eplans.com

2 Bedrooms | **2 Full Baths**

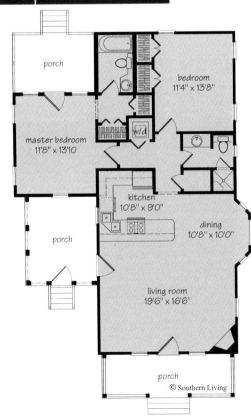

porch

bedroom
11'4" x 13'8"

master bedroom
11'8" x 13'10"

w/d

kitchen
10'8" x 9'0"

dining
10'8" x 10'0"

porch

living room
19'6" x 16'6"

porch

© Southern Living

Southern Living Style

Foxglove Cottage

1,087 square feet

ARCHITECTURAL RENDERING: LYNETTE GIROURARD

1 *Bedroom* | 1 *Full Bath*

PLAN #HPK3400081

Designed by John Tee, Architect

First Floor: 631 sq. ft.

Second Floor: 456 sq. ft.

Total: 1,087 sq. ft.

Width: 38' - 4"

Depth: 30' - 0"

Foundation: Unfinished Basement

1-800-850-1491
eplans.com

master bedroom 14'4" x 15'2"

Second Floor

great room 19'7" x 13'4"

screen porch

kitchen 11'4" x 8'8"

dining 14'0" x 10'0"

porch

© Southern Living

First Floor

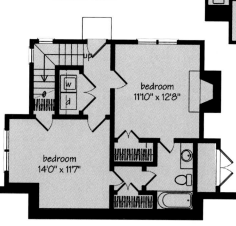

bedroom 11'10" x 12'8"

bedroom 14'0" x 11'7"

Optional Basement Level

Fox River

PLAN #HPK3400020

Designed by William H. Phillips

First Floor: 870 sq. ft.

Second Floor: 252 sq. ft.

Total: 1,122 sq. ft.

Width: 34' - 0"

Depth: 34' - 0"

Foundation: Crawlspace

1-800-850-1491
eplans.com

2 *Bedrooms* | 2 *Full Baths*

master bedroom
11' x 18'8"

dining room
11'8" x 8'10"

kitchen
10' x 11'10"

living room
15'8" x 9'3"

up

porch

© Southern Living

First Floor

loft/bedroom
15'9" x 11'8"

dn.

Second Floor

Southern Living *Style*

Hunting Creek Alternate

2 *Bedrooms* | 2 *Full Baths*

PLAN #HPK3400018

Designed by William H. Phillips

First Floor: 896 sq. ft.

Second Floor: 269 sq. ft.

Total: 1,165 sq. ft.

Width: 38' - 6"

Depth: 45' - 2"

Foundation: Crawlspace

1-800-850-1491
eplans.com

bedroom
14'6" x 11'6"

porch

up

living room
12'2" x 16'4"

w/d

dining room
17'10" x 10'0"

kitchen
12'3" x 7'8"

porch

© Southern Living

First Floor

bedroom
14'4" x 10'0"

open to
below

dn

Second Floor

Chestnut Lane

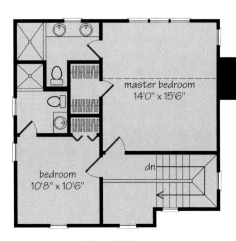

PLAN #HPK3400080

Designed by Sullivan Design Company

First Floor: 630 sq. ft.

Second Floor: 543 sq. ft.

Total: 1,173 sq. ft.

Width: 25' – 8"

Depth: 43' – 2"

Foundation: Crawlspace

1-800-850-1491
eplans.com

| 2 Bedrooms | 2 Full Baths | 1 Half Bath |

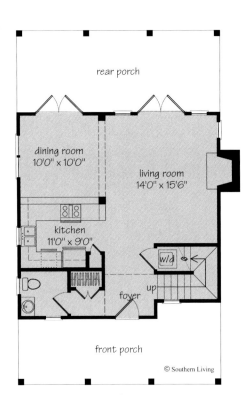

rear porch

dining room
10'0" x 10'0"

living room
14'0" x 15'6"

kitchen
11'0" x 9'0"

w/d

foyer

up

front porch

© Southern Living

First Floor

master bedroom
14'0" x 15'6"

bedroom
10'8" x 10'6"

dn

Second Floor

ARCHITECTURAL RENDERING: ROLAND DAVIS

2 *Bedrooms* | 2 *Full Baths*

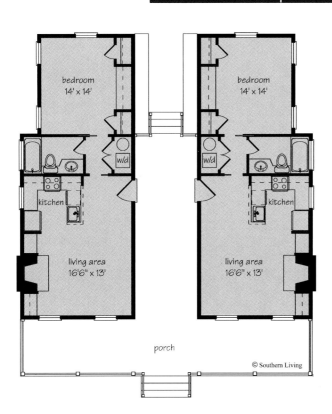

bedroom
14' x 14'

bedroom
14' x 14'

w/d

w/d

kitchen

kitchen

living area
16'6" x 13'

living area
16'6" x 13'

porch

© Southern Living

Sweetwater

PLAN #HPK3400030

Designed by William H. Phillips

First Floor: 787 sq. ft.

Second Floor: 470 sq. ft.

Total: 1,257 sq. ft.

Width: 28' - 6"

Depth: 39' - 6"

Foundation: Crawlspace

1-800-850-1491
eplans.com

1 *Bedroom* | 2 *Full Baths*

porch

kitchen/dining
21' x 10'

living room
18'11" x 21'6"

© Southern Living

up

porch

First Floor

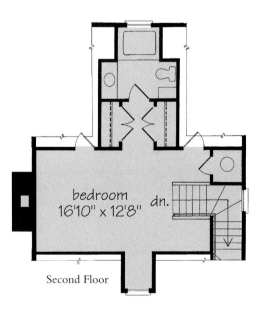

bedroom
16'10" x 12'8"   dn.

Second Floor

Banning Court

2 *Bedrooms* | 2 *Full Baths*

PLAN #HPK3400008

Designed by Moser Design Group

Square Footage: 1,286

Width: 39' - 7"

Depth: 57' - 6"

Foundation: Crawlspace

1-800-850-1491
eplans.com

porch

master bedroom
12'8" x 15'0"

w
d

den/bedroom
11'0" x 12'0"

kitchen
10'0" x 13'8"

dining
11'0" x 11'0"

screen
porch

library
8'4" x 11'6"

living room
18'8" x 15'6"

porch

© Southern Living

Nautical Cottage

ARCHITECTURAL RENDERING: MILES MELTON

PLAN #HPK3400119

Designed by Scott Ziegler

First Floor: 960 sq. ft.

Second Floor: 355 sq. ft.

Total: 1,315 sq. ft.

Width: 36' - 0"

Depth: 49' - 0"

Foundation: Crawlspace

1-800-850-1491
eplans.com

3 *Bedrooms* | 2 *Full Baths*

loft

open to below

master bedroom
10'10" x 15'

dn.

Second Floor

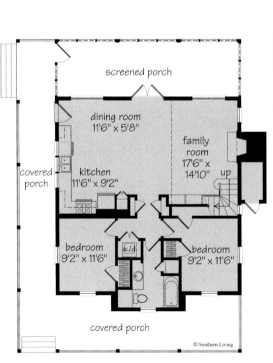

screened porch

dining room
11'6" x 5'8"

family room
17'6" x 14'10"

covered porch

kitchen
11'6" x 9'2"

up

w./d.

bedroom
9'2" x 11'6"

bedroom
9'2" x 11'6"

covered porch

© Southern Living

First Floor

Caribbean Getaway

RENDERING: MUIR STEWART

| 2 *Bedrooms* | 2 *Full Baths* | 1 *Half Bath* |

PLAN #HPK3400075

Designed by William H. Phillips for Coastal Living Magazine

First Floor: 693 sq. ft.

Second Floor: 643 sq. ft.

Total: 1,336 sq. ft.

Width: 29' - 0"

Depth: 41' - 0"

Foundation: Slab

1-800-850-1491
eplans.com

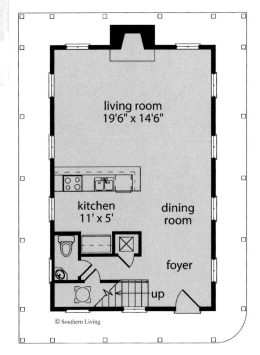

© Southern Living

First Floor

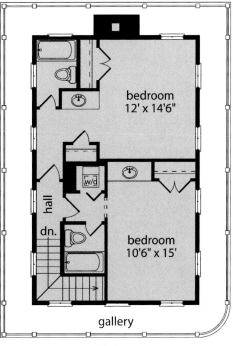

Second Floor

Rustic Beach Cottage

ARCHITECTURAL RENDERING: MUIR STEWART

MUIR STEWART

PLAN #HPK3400050

Designed by John Tee, Architect for
Coastal Living Magazine

2 *Bedrooms* | 2 *Full Baths*

First Floor: 1,030 sq. ft.

Second Floor: 368 sq. ft.

Total: 1,398 sq. ft.

Width: 46' - 0"

Depth: 40' - 0"

Foundation: Crawlspace

1-800-850-1491
eplans.com

deck

dining room
13' x 12'6"

up

screened porch

family room
15'6" x 23'

kitchen
11' x 9"

w.
d.

bedroom
12' x 15'4"

porch

© Southern Living

First Floor

master
bedroom
13'4" x 15'

open
to below

dn.

Second Floor

Spinnerbait Retreat

3 Bedrooms	2 Full Baths	1 Half Bath

PLAN #HPK3400115

Designed by Caldwell-Cline Architects and Designers for Reynolds Landing

First Floor: 721 sq. ft.

Second Floor: 687 sq. ft.

Total: 1,408 sq. ft.

Width: 32' - 0"

Depth: 38' - 10"

Foundation: Crawlspace

1-800-850-1491
eplans.com

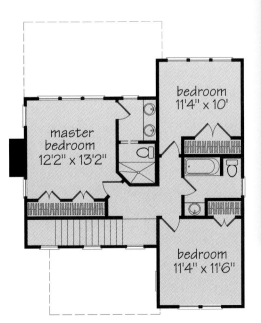

porch

b'fast room
9'4" x 11'4"

kitchen
11'4" x 11'2"

family room
17'4" x 15'6"

up

W. d.

porch

© Southern Living

First Floor

master bedroom
12'2" x 13'2"

bedroom
11'4" x 10'

bedroom
11'4" x 11'6"

Second Floor

Heather Place

ARCHITECTURAL RENDERING: LYNETTE GIROURARD

PLAN #HPK3400060

Designed by John Tee, Architect

First Floor: 890 sq. ft.

Second Floor: 596 sq. ft.

Total: 1,486 sq. ft.

Width: 49' - 4"

Depth: 30' - 0"

Foundation: Unfinished Basement

1-800-850-1491
eplans.com

3 *Bedrooms* | 2 *Full Baths* | 1 *Half Bath*

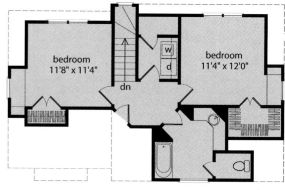

Second Floor

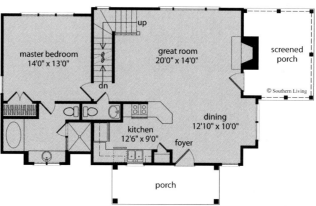

First Floor

© Southern Living

ARCHITECTURAL RENDERING: KEN PIEPER

© Southern Living

3 Bedrooms | 2 Full Baths

PLAN #HPK3400035

Designed by William H. Phillips

Square Footage: 1,500

Width: 50' - 0"

Depth: 46' - 0"

Foundation: Crawlspace

1-800-850-1491
eplans.com

coverd porch

bedroom
13'1" x 11'5"

great room
22'4" x 17'0"

master bedroom
13'1" x 15'2"

bedroom
13'1" x 11'7"

kitchen
10'9" x 11'11"

w | d

coverd porch

Forsythia

PLAN #HPK3400078

Designed by William H. Phillips

First Floor: 1,016 sq. ft.

Second Floor: 505 sq. ft.

Total: 1,521 sq. ft.

Width: 32' - 7"

Depth: 44' - 3"

Foundation: Crawlspace

1-800-850-1491
eplans.com

| 3 *Bedrooms* | 2 *Full Baths* | 1 *Half Bath* |

First Floor

Second Floor

Gardenia

1,540 square feet

3 *Bedrooms* | **2** *Full Baths* | **1** *Half Bath*

PLAN #HPK3400079

Designed by William H. Phillips

First Floor: 1,024 sq. ft.

Second Floor: 516 sq. ft.

Total: 1,540 sq. ft.

Width: 32' - 3"

Depth: 46' - 1"

Foundation: Crawlspace

1-800-850-1491
eplans.com

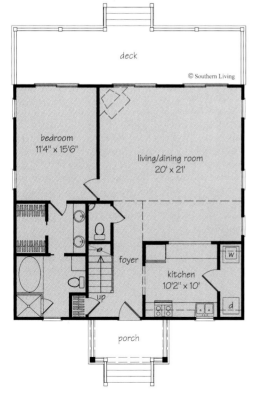

First Floor

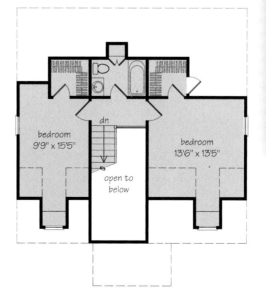

Second Floor

Hunting Creek

ARCHITECTURAL RENDERING: GREG HAVENS

PLAN #HPK3400016

Designed by William H. Phillips

First Floor: 1,128 sq. ft.

Second Floor: 457 sq. ft.

Total: 1,585 sq. ft.

Width: 38' – 6"

Depth: 45' – 2"

Foundation: Crawlspace

1-800-850-1491
eplans.com

2 *Bedrooms* | 2 *Full Baths* | 1 *Half Bath*

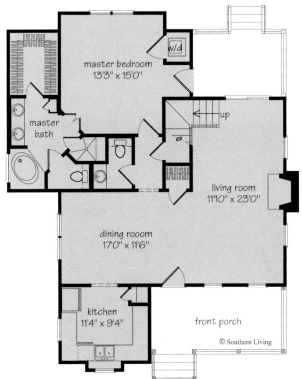

master bedroom
13'3" x 15'0"

w/d

master bath

up

living room
11'10" x 23'0"

dining rooom
17'0" x 11'6"

kitchen
11'4" x 9'4"

front porch

© Southern Living

First Floor

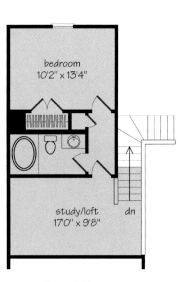

bedroom
10'2" x 13'4"

study/loft
17'0" x 9'8"

dn

Second Floor

Ashley River Cottage

ARCHITECTURAL RENDERING: RICK HERR

3 *Bedrooms* | **2** *Full Baths* | **1** *Half Bath*

PLAN #HPK3400009

Designed by Allison-Ramsey Architects, Inc.

First Floor: 1,093 sq. ft.

Second Floor: 512 sq. ft.

Total: 1,605 sq. ft.

Width: 32' - 4"

Depth: 50' - 4"

Foundation: Pier (same as Piling)

1-800-850-1491
eplans.com

master bedroom 14' x 16'

screened porch

w.

up

kitchen 9'8" x 14'4"

service

living room 16' x 14'

dining room 13'4" x 10'

porch

© Southern Living

First Floor

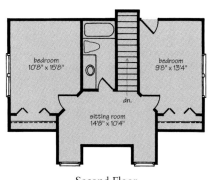

bedroom 10'8" x 15'8"

bedroom 9'8" x 13'4"

dn.

sitting room 14'8" x 10'4"

Second Floor

Ellsworth Cottage

ARCHITECTURAL RENDERING: RICHARD CHENOWETH

PLAN #HPK3400036

Designed by Caldwell-Cline Architects for Cottage Living Magazine

First Floor: 1,135 sq. ft.

Second Floor: 510 sq. ft.

Total: 1,645 sq. ft.

Width: 37' - 10"

Depth: 49' - 5"

Foundation: Unfinished Basement

1-800-850-1491
eplans.com

3 *Bedrooms* | 2 *Full Baths* | 1 *Half Bath*

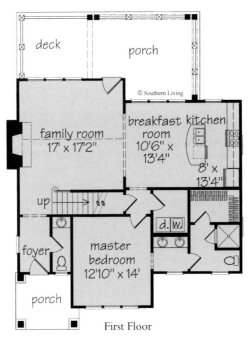

First Floor

deck
porch
family room 17' x 17'2"
breakfast room 10'6" x 13'4"
kitchen
8' x 13'4"
© Southern Living
up
foyer
master bedroom 12'10" x 14'
d. w.
porch

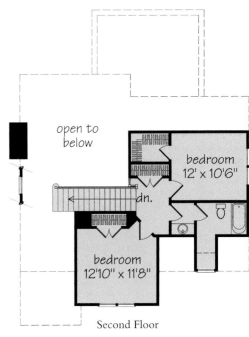

Second Floor

open to below
bedroom 12' x 10'6"
dn.
bedroom 12'10" x 11'8"

Sage House

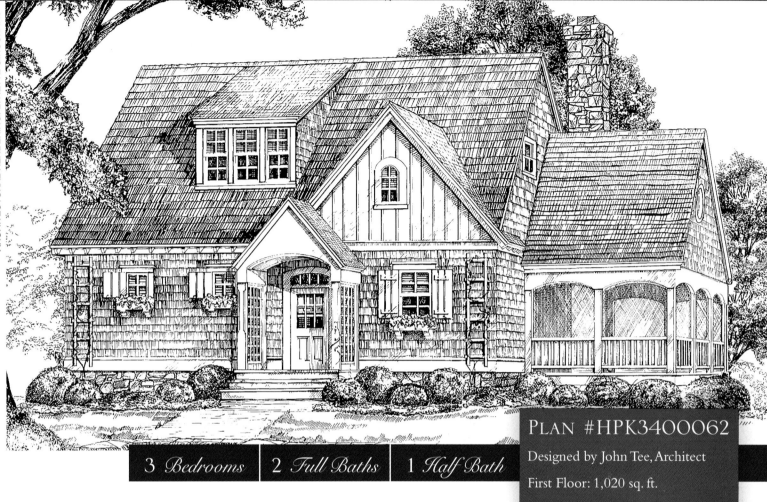

| 3 Bedrooms | 2 Full Baths | 1 Half Bath |

PLAN #HPK3400062

Designed by John Tee, Architect

First Floor: 1,020 sq. ft.

Second Floor: 643 sq. ft.

Total: 1,663 sq. ft.

Width: 34' - 0"

Depth: 30' - 0"

Foundation: Unfinished Basement

1-800-850-1491
eplans.com

master bedroom
13'2" x 14'

family room
16'2" x 14'

screened
porch

dining room
16'2" x 7'

up

dn.

w./d.

foyer

kitchen
11'10" x 7'8"

porch

© Southern Living

First Floor

bedroom
12' x 11'10"

bedroom
15' x 11'10"

computer room
17'0" x 7'6"

dn.

Second Floor

Stripers Cottage

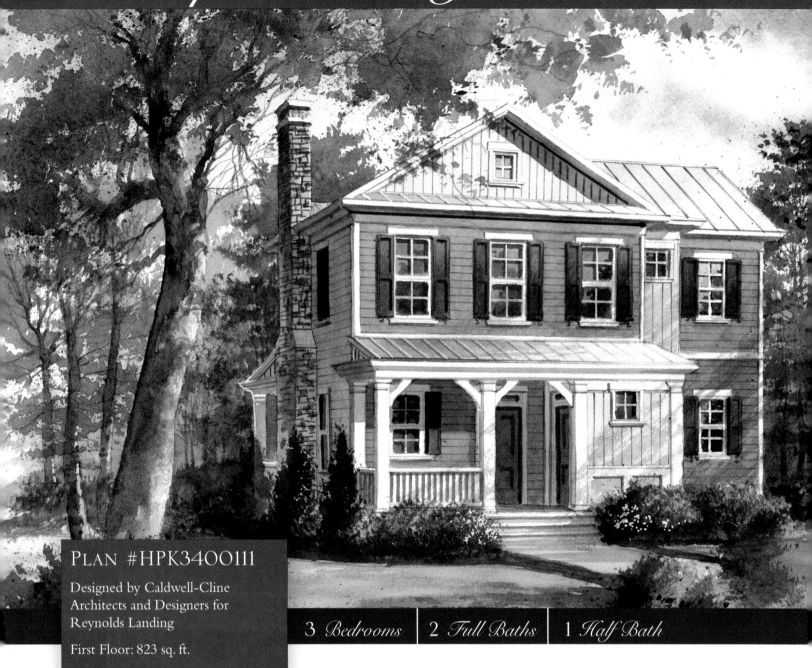

PLAN #HPK3400111

Designed by Caldwell-Cline
Architects and Designers for
Reynolds Landing

First Floor: 823 sq. ft.

Second Floor: 855 sq. ft.

Total: 1,678 sq. ft.

Width: 34' - 6"

Depth: 41' - 0"

Foundation: Crawlspace

1-800-850-1491
eplans.com

3 *Bedrooms* | 2 *Full Baths* | 1 *Half Bath*

STRIPERS COTTAGE has the unique appeal of an
old homestead that has grown throughout the decades, yet
it is as open and efficient as if it were built just yesterday.
A small porch on the front of the home provides requisite
visual charm; a larger porch at the rear provides a place to
while away warm afternoons. A stone hearth warms the
family room inside, as well as the open L-shaped kitchen
and adjacent dining area. Upstairs, the master bedroom
features a dual-sink bath and walk-in closet. Windows on
two walls enhance the space. ✺

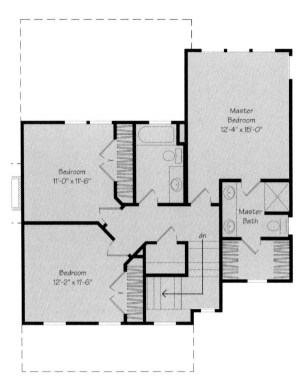

Bedroom
11'-0" x 11'-6"

Master
Bedroom
12'-4" x 15'-0"

Master
Bath

Bedroom
12'-2" x 11'-6"

dn

Second Floor

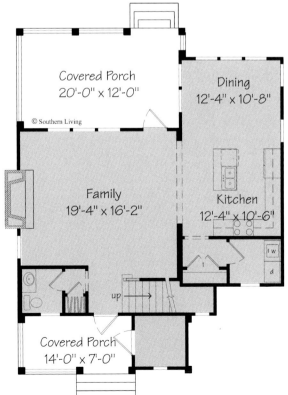

Covered Porch
20'-0" x 12'-0"

© Southern Living

Dining
12'-4" x 10'-8"

Family
19'-4" x 16'-2"

Kitchen
12'-4" x 10'-6"

w

d

up

Covered Porch
14'-0" x 7'-0"

First Floor

Coosaw River Cottage

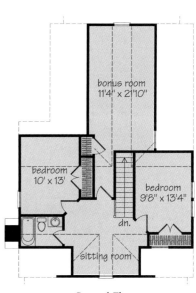

ARCHITECTURAL RENDERING: KEN PIEPER

PLAN #HPK3400056

Designed by Allison-Ramsey Architects, Inc.

First Floor: 1,195 sq. ft.

Second Floor: 510 sq. ft.

Total: 1,705 sq. ft.

Bonus Space: 290 sq. ft.

Width: 32' - 4"

Depth: 58' - 4"

Foundation: Crawlspace

1-800-850-1491
eplans.com

| 3 Bedrooms | 2 Full Baths | 1 Half Bath |

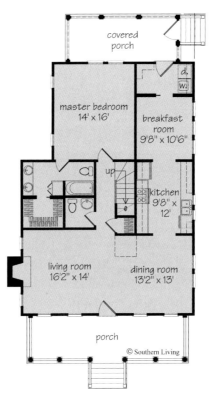

First Floor

Second Floor

© Southern Living

Tidewater Cottage

4 Bedrooms | **2 Full Baths**

PLAN #HPK3400063

Designed by Looney Ricks Kiss Architects, Inc. for Coastal Living Magazine

First Floor: 975 sq. ft.

Second Floor: 643 sq. ft.

Third Floor: 92 sq. ft.

Total: 1,710 sq. ft.

Width: 32' - 5"

Depth: 47' - 0"

Foundation: Pier (same as Piling)

1-800-850-1491
eplans.com

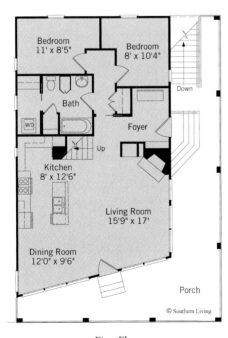

First Floor

Bedroom 11' x 8'5"

Bedroom 8' x 10'4"

Bath

Down

Foyer

Kitchen 8' x 12'6"

Up

Living Room 15'9" x 17'

Dining Room 12'0" x 9'6"

Porch

© Southern Living

Second Floor

Bunk Room 15'8" x 6'3"

Down

Up

Bath

Master Bedroom 12' x 12'

Storage

Third Floor

Down

Loft 6'5" x 12'9"

Ashton

ARCHITECTURAL RENDERING: MILES MELTON

PLAN #HPK3400010

Designed by Caldwell-Cline Architects

3 Bedrooms | 2 Full Baths | 1 Half Bath

First Floor: 1,203 sq. ft.

Second Floor: 512 sq. ft.

Total: 1,715 sq. ft.

Width: 63' - 10"

Depth: 46' - 0"

Foundation: Crawlspace, Slab, Unfinished Basement

1-800-850-1491
eplans.com

First Floor

- deck
- covered porch
- dining/breakfast 11'4" x 12'0"
- master bedroom 13'4" x 14'0"
- sleeping porch 10'0" x 14'0"
- great room 19'4" x 18'0"
- kitchen 11'4" x 10'6"
- w d
- entry
- up
- dn
- carriage house
- covered porch
- storage

© Southern Living

Second Floor

- bedroom 12'0" x 12'0"
- open to below
- bedroom 11'8" x 12'6"
- dn

ARCHITECTURAL RENDERING: RICHARD CHENOWETH

3 *Bedrooms* | 2 *Full Baths* | 1 *Half Bath*

PLAN #HPK3400043

Designed by Allison-Ramsey Architects, Inc. for Cottage Living Magazine

First Floor: 1,101 sq. ft.

Second Floor: 619 sq. ft.

Total: 1,720 sq. ft.

Width: 28' - 0"

Depth: 61' - 0"

Foundation: Crawlspace

1-800-850-1491
eplans.com

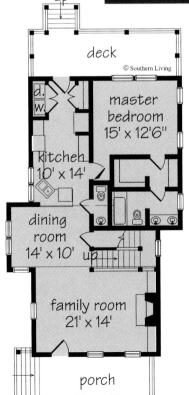

up

deck

© Southern Living

d. w

master bedroom
15' x 12'6"

kitchen
10' x 14'

dining room
14' x 10'

up

family room
21' x 14'

porch

First Floor

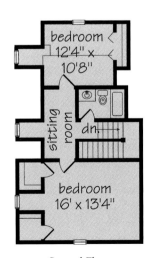

bedroom
12'4" x 10'8"

sitting room

dn

bedroom
16' x 13'4"

Second Floor

Silverhill

Lois Watson '99

PLAN #HPK3400129

Designed by Sullivan Design Company

First Floor: 1,154 sq. ft.

Second Floor: 621 sq. ft.

Total: 1,775 sq. ft.

Width: 44' - 0"

Depth: 49' - 0"

Foundation: Crawlspace

1-800-850-1491
eplans.com

3 *Bedrooms*	2 *Full Baths*	1 *Half Bath*

First Floor

- screen porch
- living room 15'4" x 13'4"
- dining room 12'4" x 11'4"
- master bedroom 15'4" x 13'4"
- up
- kitchen 11'2" x 11'8"
- w d
- foyer
- porch

© Southern Living

Second Floor

- bedroom 12'0" x 11'0"
- dn
- bedroom 13'4" x 11'4"

Bucksport Cottage

1,794 square feet

ARCHITECTURAL RENDERING: MILES MELTON

3 Bedrooms | **2 Full Baths** | **1 Half Bath**

PLAN #HPK3400021

Designed by Moser Design Group

First Floor: 1,066 sq. ft.

Second Floor: 728 sq. ft.

Total: 1,794 sq. ft.

Width: 38' - 0"

Depth: 43' - 4"

Foundation: Crawlspace

1-800-850-1491
eplans.com

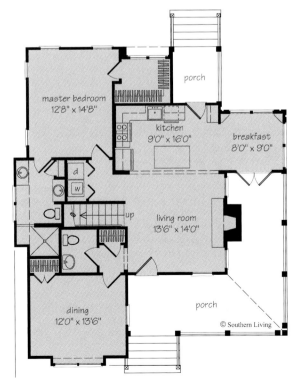

First Floor

Second Floor

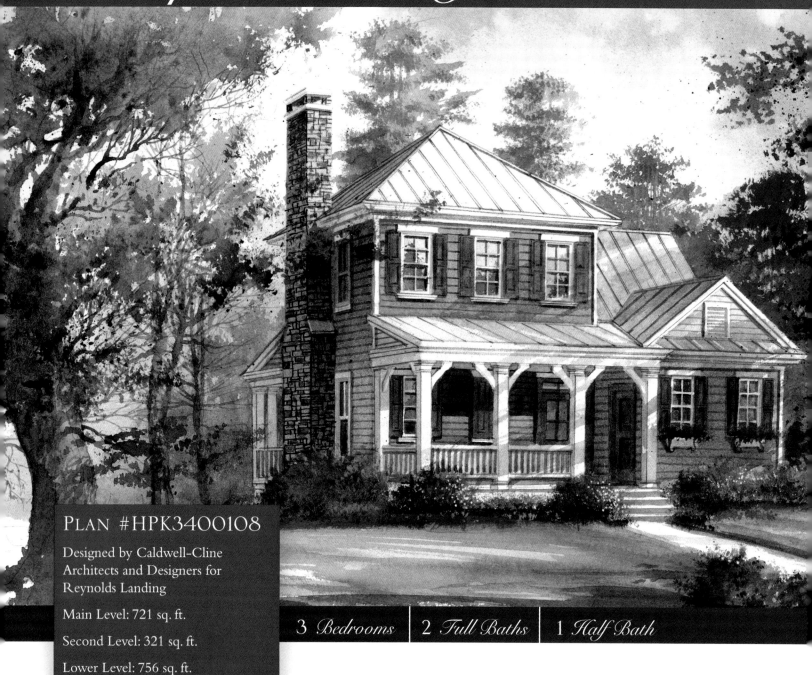

1,798 square feet

Topwater Lodge

PLAN #HPK3400108

Designed by Caldwell-Cline Architects and Designers for Reynolds Landing

Main Level: 721 sq. ft.

Second Level: 321 sq. ft.

Lower Level: 756 sq. ft.

Total: 1,798 sq. ft.

Width: 32' - 0"

Depth: 38' - 10"

Foundation: Finished Walkout Basement

1-800-850-1491
eplans.com

3 *Bedrooms* | 2 *Full Baths* | 1 *Half Bath*

TRADITIONAL PORCHES at the front and rear of the home communicate the casual, neighborly quality of this under-1,800-square-foot home. Inside, the family room is the home's main gathering space, with a conversation area anchored by the large fireplace and access to the rear porch. Nearby, the kitchen and breakfast area work closely together, providing sunlit spaces for meals and family interaction. The second floor is reserved for the master suite, comprising a full bath with vanities, walk-in closet, and windows facing the rear property. ❀

Master
Bath

Master
Bedroom
12'-2" x 15'-3"

Second Level

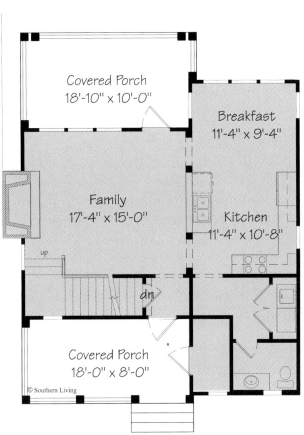

Covered Porch
18'-10" x 10'-0"

Breakfast
11'-4" x 9'-4"

Family
17'-4" x 15'-0"

Kitchen
11'-4" x 10'-8"

up

dn

Covered Porch
18'-0" x 8'-0"

© Southern Living

Main Level

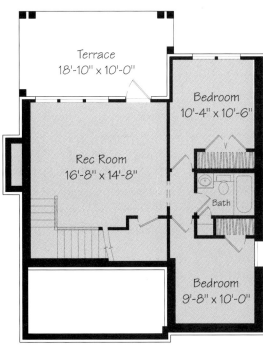

Terrace
18'-10" x 10'-0"

Bedroom
10'-4" x 10'-6"

Rec Room
16'-8" x 14'-8"

Bath

Bedroom
9'-8" x 10'-0"

Lower Level

Wisteria - Cottage E

PLAN #HPK3400061

Designed by John Tee, Architect

First Floor: 1,108 sq. ft.

Second Floor: 694 sq. ft.

Total: 1,802 sq. ft.

Width: 44' - 0"

Depth: 36' - 0"

Foundation: Unfinished Basement

1-800-850-1491
eplans.com

| 3 Bedrooms | 2 Full Baths | 1 Half Bath |

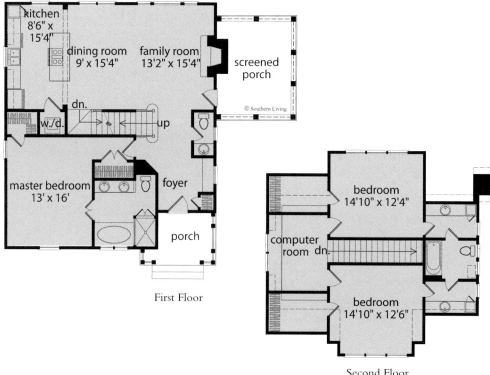

kitchen 8'6" x 15'4"

dining room 9' x 15'4"

family room 13'2" x 15'4"

screened porch

© Southern Living

dn.

w./d.

up

master bedroom 13' x 16'

foyer

porch

First Floor

bedroom 14'10" x 12'4"

computer room

dn.

bedroom 14'10" x 12'6"

Second Floor

Capeside Cottage

1,825 square feet

3 *Bedrooms* | 3 *Full Baths*

PLAN #HPK3400083

Designed by Spitzmiller and Norris, Inc.

First Floor: 1,320 sq. ft.

Second Floor: 505 sq. ft.

Total: 1,825 sq. ft.

Optional Guest Cottage: 526 sq. ft.

Width: 57' - 8"

Depth: 73' - 4"

Foundation: Pier (same as Piling)

1-800-850-1491
eplans.com

optional guest cottage
18'1" x 18'9"

covered loggia

bedroom
10'3" x 10'10"

laundry
w. d.

up

family room
16'3" x 16'6"

kitchen
13'7" x 11'2"

master bedroom
11'5" x 12'7"

dining room
11'5" x 9'11"

covered porch
20'1" x 16'

boardwalk

© Southern Living

First Floor

dn.

loft area

bedroom
11'3" x 13'10"

Second Floor

Skitter Creek Cottage

PLAN #HPK3400104

Designed by John Tee, Architect for Reynolds Landing

First Floor: 1,094 sq. ft.

Second Floor: 732 sq. ft.

Total: 1,826 sq. ft.

Width: 44' - 5"

Depth: 42' - 0"

Foundation: Crawlspace, Unfinished Basement

1-800-850-1491
eplans.com

3 *Bedrooms* | 3 *Full Baths* | 1 *Half Bath*

Second Floor

Bedroom 13'-0" x 12'-8"

Play Room 8'-10" x 10'-8"

Bedroom 13'-0" x 12'-8"

First Floor

Dining 8'-2" x 15'-8"

Great Room 14'-0" x 15'-8"

Kitchen 8'-6" x 15'-8"

Screen Porch 12'-5" x 20'-6"

Master Bedroom 13'-2" x 15'-8"

Master Bath

Foyer

Covered Porch

© Southern Living

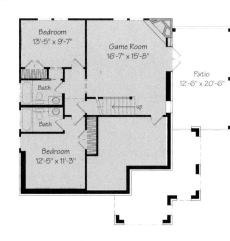

Bedroom 13'-5" x 9'-7"

Game Room 16'-7" x 15'-8"

Bath

Bath

Patio 12'-6" x 20'-6"

Bedroom 12'-5" x 11'-3"

Shad Shack Retreat

1,826 square feet

3 Bedrooms | 3 Full Baths | 1 Half Bath

PLAN #HPK3400105

Designed by John Tee, Architect for Reynolds Landing

First Floor: 1,094 sq. ft.

Second Floor: 732 sq. ft.

Total: 1,826 sq. ft.

Width: 44' – 5"

Depth: 42' – 0"

Foundation: Crawlspace, Finished Walkout Basement

1-800-850-1491
eplans.com

Second Floor

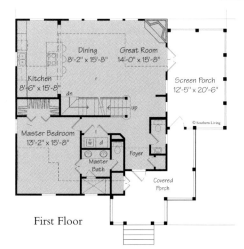

First Floor

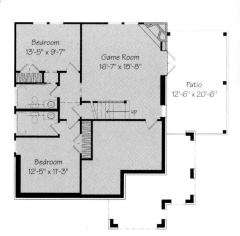

Gresham Creek Cottage

ARCHITECTURAL RENDERING: MILES MELTON

PLAN #HPK3400024

Designed by Moser Design Group

First Floor: 1,350 sq. ft.

Second Floor: 481 sq. ft.

Total: 1,831 sq. ft.

Width: 37' - 7"

Depth: 57' - 2"

Foundation: Crawlspace

1-800-850-1491
eplans.com

3 *Bedrooms* | **2** *Full Baths* | **1** *Half Bath*

First Floor

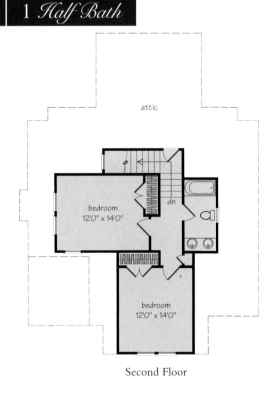

Second Floor

Jasmine

ARCHITECTURAL RENDERING: ROLAND DAVIS

3 *Bedrooms* | 2 *Full Baths* | 1 *Half Bath*

PLAN #HPK3400126

Designed by William H. Phillips

First Floor: 1,092 sq. ft.

Second Floor: 750 sq. ft.

Total: 1,842 sq. ft.

Width: 44' - 0"

Depth: 41' - 0"

Foundation: Crawlspace

1-800-850-1491
eplans.com

deck

master bedroom 12' x 11'6"

living room 14' x 16'

dining room 10' x 13'

w. d.

foyer

kitchen 12' x 9'

up

porch

© Southern Living

First Floor

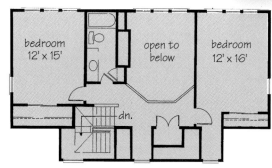

bedroom 12' x 15'

open to below

bedroom 12' x 16'

dn.

Second Floor

Fly-Ty Retreat

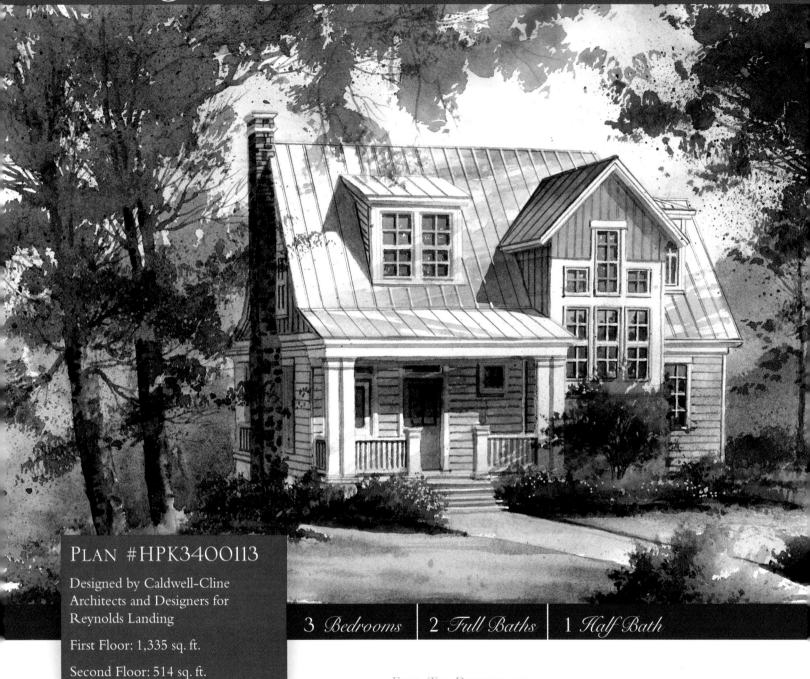

PLAN #HPK3400113

Designed by Caldwell-Cline
Architects and Designers for
Reynolds Landing

First Floor: 1,335 sq. ft.

Second Floor: 514 sq. ft.

Total: 1,849 sq. ft.

Width: 44' - 6"

Depth: 52' - 0"

Foundation: Crawlspace

1-800-850-1491
eplans.com

3 *Bedrooms* | 2 *Full Baths* | 1 *Half Bath*

FLY-TY RETREAT looks like the quintessential little
vacation cottage, with the surprisingly beautiful addition of a
cathedral-windowed stairwell rising through the front of the
home and bringing light to the dining area below. The main
level provides an abundance of wide-open gathering space,
loosely divided into family room, dining room, and efficient
kitchen. The master bedroom at the back allows the hosts
to enjoy some privacy while guests are cozy in the uniquely
shaped bedrooms upstairs. And like any great vacation retreat,
there is plenty of outdoor living space! ✤

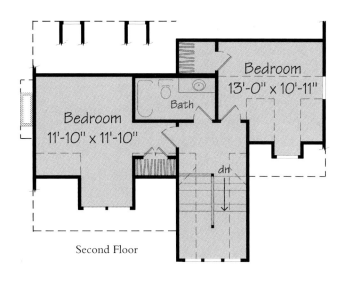

Bedroom
11'-10" x 11'-10"

Bath

Bedroom
13'-0" x 10'-11"

dn

Second Floor

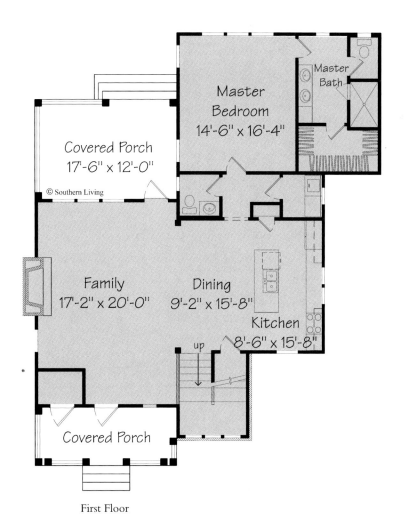

Covered Porch
17'-6" x 12'-0"

Master
Bedroom
14'-6" x 16'-4"

Master
Bath

© Southern Living

Family
17'-2" x 20'-0"

Dining
9'-2" x 15'-8"

Kitchen
8'-6" x 15'-8"

up

Covered Porch

First Floor

Piedmont Cottage

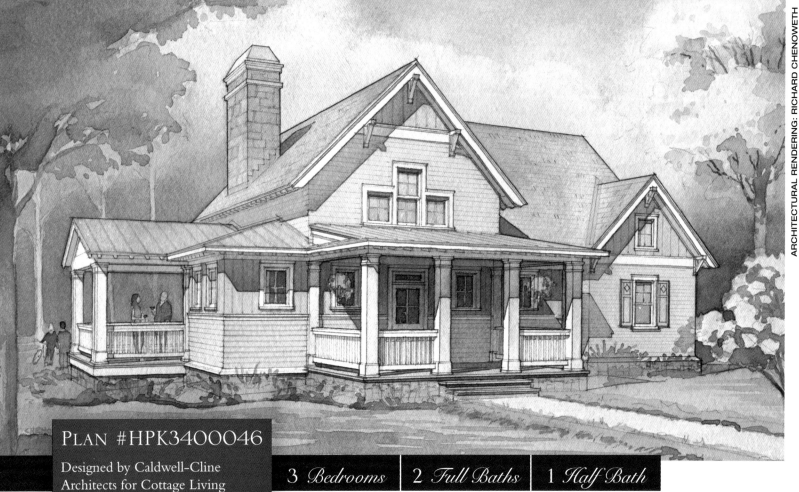

ARCHITECTURAL RENDERING: RICHARD CHENOWETH

PLAN #HPK3400046

Designed by Caldwell-Cline Architects for Cottage Living Magazine

First Floor: 1,338 sq. ft.

Second Floor: 517 sq. ft.

Total: 1,855 sq. ft.

Width: 58' - 9"

Depth: 44' - 5"

Foundation: Unfinished Basement

1-800-850-1491
eplans.com

3 *Bedrooms* | 2 *Full Baths* | 1 *Half Bath*

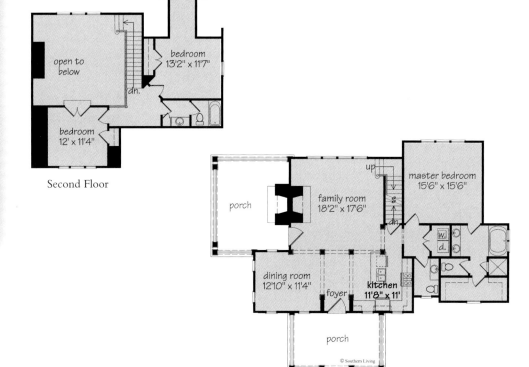

Second Floor

First Floor

Turtle Lake Cottage

1,871 square feet

| 3 *Bedrooms* | 2 *Full Baths* | 1 *Half Bath* |

PLAN #HPK3400070

Designed by Moser Design Group

First Floor: 1,308 sq. ft.

Second Floor: 563 sq. ft.

Total: 1,871 sq. ft.

Width: 42' – 0"

Depth: 63' – 4"

Foundation: Crawlspace

1-800-850-1491
eplans.com

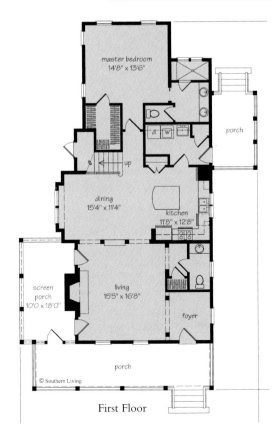

master bedroom
14'8" x 13'6"

porch

dining
15'4" x 11'4"

kitchen
11'8" x 12'8"

screen
porch
10'0" x 18'0"

living
15'5" x 16'8"

foyer

porch

© Southern Living

First Floor

bedroom
14'0" x 11'6"

bedroom
15'6" x 11'4"

Second Floor

Winonna Park

PLAN #HPK3400122

Designed by Circa Studios

First Floor: 1,174 sq. ft.

Second Floor: 698 sq. ft.

Total: 1,872 sq. ft.

Width: 30' - 0"

Depth: 45' - 9"

Foundation: Crawlspace

1-800-850-1491
eplans.com

3 *Bedrooms* | 2 *Full Baths*

Second Floor

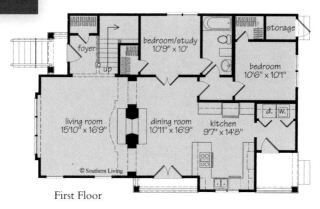

First Floor

River Cliff Cottage

ARCHITECTURAL RENDERING: MILES MELTON

3 *Bedrooms* | **3** *Full Baths* | **1** *Half Bath*

PLAN #HPK3400058

Designed by Mouzon Design

First Floor: 1,288 sq. ft.

Second Floor: 622 sq. ft.

Total: 1,910 sq. ft.

Width: 38' – 0"

Depth: 73' – 2"

Foundation: Crawlspace

1-800-850-1491
eplans.com

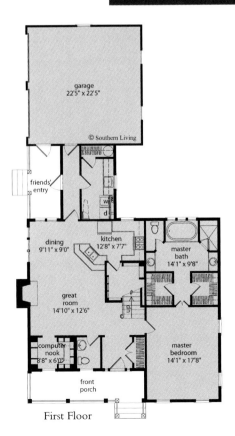

First Floor

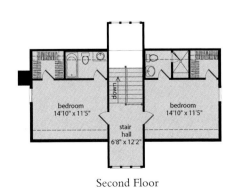

Second Floor

Twitchin Minnow

PLAN #HPK3400100

Designed by John Tee, Architect for Reynolds Landing

First Floor: 1,208 sq. ft.

Second Floor: 712 sq. ft.

Total: 1,920 sq. ft.

Width: 44' - 0"

Depth: 46' - 0"

Foundation: Crawlspace, Unfinished Basement

1-800-850-1491
eplans.com

| 3 Bedrooms | 3 Full Baths | 1 Half Bath |

THOUGH RUSTIC IN APPEARANCE, the Twitchin Minnow provides all the amenities required to vacation in style. Situate it on a gentle slope to make the most of the various porches and terraces that extend from the front, rear, and walkout basement. Imagine every comfortable seat indoors and out, filled with family and friends...chatting, laughing, or curled up with books. The wide-open gathering spaces are balanced by numerous bedrooms, most with their own baths, because everybody enjoys a private retreat while on vacation. ❈

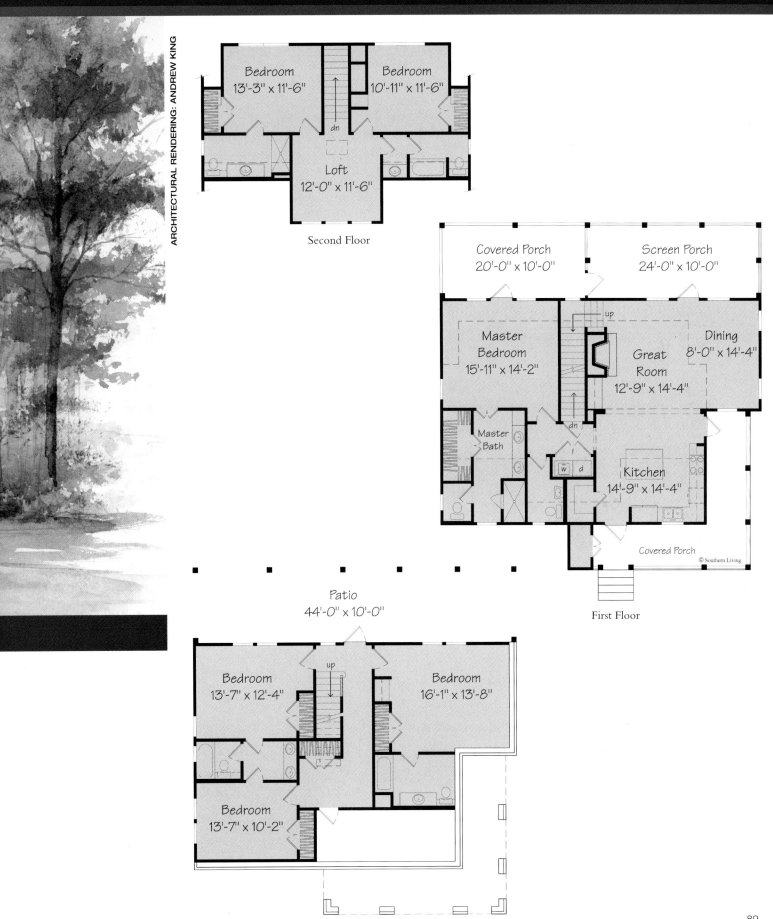

Bedroom
13'-3" x 11'-6"

Bedroom
10'-11" x 11'-6"

dn

Loft
12'-0" x 11'-6"

Second Floor

Covered Porch
20'-0" x 10'-0"

Screen Porch
24'-0" x 10'-0"

up

Master Bedroom
15'-11" x 14'-2"

Dining
8'-0" x 14'-4"

Great Room
12'-9" x 14'-4"

Master Bath

dn

w   d

Kitchen
14'-9" x 14'-4"

Covered Porch

© Southern Living

First Floor

Patio
44'-0" x 10'-0"

up

Bedroom
13'-7" x 12'-4"

Bedroom
16'-1" x 13'-8"

Bedroom
13'-7" x 10'-2"

1,920 square feet

Lil Popper

ARCHITECTURAL RENDERING: ANDREW KING

PLAN #HPK3400101

Designed by John Tee, Architect for Reynolds Landing

First Floor: 1,208 sq. ft.

Second Floor: 712 sq. ft.

Total: 1,920 sq. ft.

Width: 44' - 0"

Depth: 46' - 0"

Foundation: Crawlspace, Unfinished Basement

1-800-850-1491
eplans.com

3 Bedrooms | *3 Full Baths* | *1 Half Bath*

Covered Porch
20'-0" x 10'-0"

Screen Porch
24'-0" x 10'-0"

up

Master Bedroom
15'-11" x 14'-2"

Great Room
12'-9" x 14'-4"

Dining
8'-0" x 14'-4"

Master Bath

dn

w | d

Kitchen
14'-9" x 14'-4"

Covered Porch

© Southern Living

First Floor

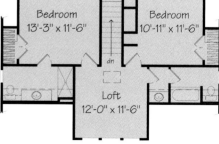

Bedroom
13'-3" x 11'-6"

Bedroom
10'-11" x 11'-6"

dn

Loft
12'-0" x 11'-6"

Second Floor

ARCHITECTURAL RENDERING: MUIR STEWART

| 4 *Bedrooms* | 3 *Full Baths* |

PLAN #HPK3400057

Designed by Sullivan Design Company for Coastal Living Magazine

First Floor: 1,016 sq. ft.

Second Floor: 911 sq. ft.

Total: 1,927 sq. ft.

Width: 40' - 0"

Depth: 50' - 8"

Foundation: Crawlspace

1-800-850-1491
eplans.com

Second Floor

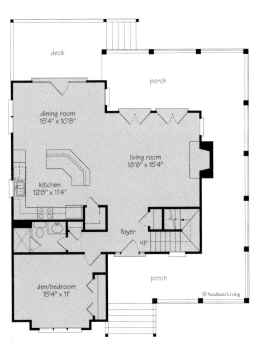

First Floor

1,938 square feet

Elizabeths Place

PLAN #HPK3400022

Designed by Mitchell Ginn

First Floor: 983 sq. ft.

Second Floor: 955 sq. ft.

Total: 1,938 sq. ft.

Width: 69' - 8"

Depth: 42' - 10"

Foundation: Unfinished Basement

1-800-850-1491
eplans.com

3 *Bedrooms* | 2 *Full Baths* | 1 *Half Bath*

garage
23'4" x 21'4"

© Southern Living

deck

screened porch
10'0" x 11'4"

eating
14'0" x 12'4"

family room
16'2" x 13'4"

kitchen
14'0" x 11'8"

up

foyer

dining
14'0" x 14'10"

porch

First Floor

bedroom
11'2" x 12'0"

bedroom
11'2" x 11'0"

dn

master bedroom
14'0" x 14'10"

w
d

Second Floor

Bucketmouth Bungalow

| 3 Bedrooms | 3 Full Baths | 1 Half Bath |

PLAN #HPK3400106

Designed by John Tee, Architect for Reynolds Landing

Main Level: 1,094 sq. ft.

Lower Level: 876 sq. ft.

Total: 1,970 sq. ft.

Width: 44' - 5"

Depth: 42' - 0"

Foundation: Finished Walkout Basement

1-800-850-1491
eplans.com

Main Level

Lower Level

Cricket Cottage

PLAN #HPK3400107

Designed by John Tee, Architect for Reynolds Landing

3 Bedrooms | **3 Full Baths** | **1 Half Bath**

Main Level: 1,094 sq. ft.

Lower Level: 876 sq. ft.

Total: 1,970 sq. ft.

Width: 44' – 5"

Depth: 42' – 0"

Foundation: Finished Walkout Basement

1-800-850-1491
eplans.com

Lower Level

- Bedroom 13'-5" x 9'-10"
- Game Room 16'-7" x 15'-8"
- Patio 12'-6" x 20'-6"
- Bath
- Bath
- Bedroom 12'-5" x 11'-0"

Main Level

- Dining 8'-2" x 15'-8"
- Great Room 14'-0" x 15'-8"
- Kitchen 8'-6" x 15'-8"
- Screen Porch 12'-5" x 20'-6"
- Master Bedroom 13'-2" x 15'-8"
- Master Bath
- Foyer
- Deck
- Covered Porch

© Southern Living

Bermuda Bluff Cottage

1,998 square feet

3 *Bedrooms* | **3** *Full Baths*

PLAN #HPK3400048

Designed by Allison-Ramsey Architects, Inc. for Coastal Living Magazine

First Floor: 1,606 sq. ft.

Second Floor: 392 sq. ft.

Total: 1,998 sq. ft.

Width: 54' - 8"

Depth: 50' - 8"

Foundation: Crawlspace

1-800-850-1491
eplans.com

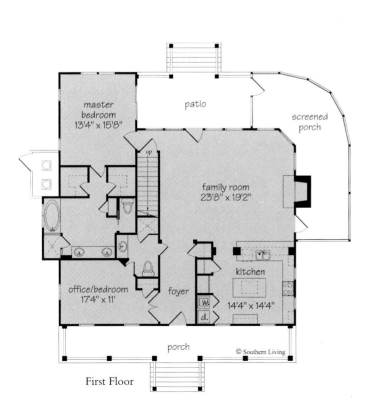

First Floor

Second Floor

2,009 square feet

Specks River Cottage

PLAN #HPK3400112

Designed by Caldwell-Cline
Architects and Designers for
Reynolds Landing

Main Level: 823 sq. ft.

Second Level: 317 sq. ft.

Lower Level: 869 sq. ft.

Total: 2,009 sq. ft.

Width: 34' – 6"

Depth: 41' – 0"

Foundation: Finished
Walkout Basement

1-800-850-1491
eplans.com

3 *Bedrooms* | 2 *Full Baths* | 1 *Half Bath*

THE MASTER SUITE IS PERCHED at
the top of Specks River Cottage, to take advantage of mountain breezes and lake views. The
arrangement also gives the hosts a sense of retreat
from guests or children, who will be snug in the
bedrooms in the walkout basement. A large sitting room and a terrace on this level make it a
retreat of its own. The main level provides plenty
of space for family and guests to gather, in front
of the broad hearth, around the kitchen island, or
outside on either of the two porches. ✤

ARCHITECTURAL RENDERING: ANDREW KING

© Southern Living

Covered Porch
20'-0" x 12'-0"

Dining
12'-4" x 9'-6"

Family
19'-6" x 16'-2"

Kitchen
12'-4" x 10'-0"

dn

W

d

up

dn

Covered Porch
14'-0" x 7'-0"

Main Level

Master Bedroom
15'-6" x 12'-2"

Master Bath

dn

Second Level

Terrace
20'-0" x 12'-0"

Bedroom
11'-0" x 11'-10"

Sitting
13'-0" x 15'-10"

Bedroom
11'-6" x 11'-0"

up

Lower Level

Whitefish Retreat

ARCHITECTURAL RENDERING: MUIR STEWART

PLAN #HPK3400116

Designed by Stephen Fuller, Inc.
for Coastal Living Magazine

3 *Bedrooms* | 2 *Full Baths*

Square Footage: 2,019

Bonus Space: 363 sq. ft.

Width: 56' - 0"

Depth: 52' - 0"

Foundation: Crawlspace

1-800-850-1491
eplans.com

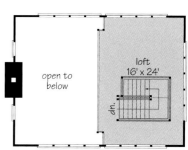

open to below

loft
16' x 24'

dn.

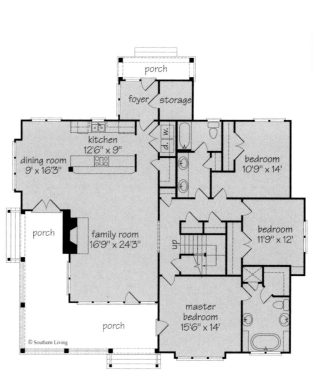

porch

foyer | storage

kitchen
12'6" x 9"

dining room
9' x 16'3"

d. w.

bedroom
10'9" x 14'

porch

family room
16'9" x 24'3"

up

bedroom
11'9" x 12'

porch

master bedroom
15'6" x 14'

© Southern Living

Spartina Cottage

MUIR STEWART '04

3 *Bedrooms* | **2** *Full Baths* | **1** *Half Bath*

PLAN #HPK3400064

Designed by George Graves, AIA
for Coastal Living Magazine

First Floor: 1,221 sq. ft.

Second Floor: 810 sq. ft.

Total: 2,031 sq. ft.

Width: 40' - 0"

Depth: 54' - 0"

Foundation: Pier (same as Piling)

1-800-850-1491
eplans.com

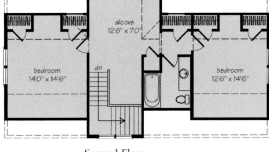

Second Floor

First Floor

Walterboro Ridge

MILES MELTON

PLAN #HPK3400071

Designed by Moser Design Group

First Floor: 1,441 sq. ft.

Second Floor: 610 sq. ft.

Total: 2,051 sq. ft.

Width: 34' - 4"

Depth: 55' - 6"

Foundation: Crawlspace

1-800-850-1491
eplans.com

3 or 4 Bedrooms | *2 Full Baths* | *1 Half Bath*

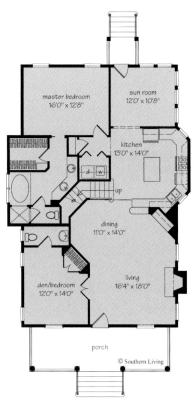

First Floor

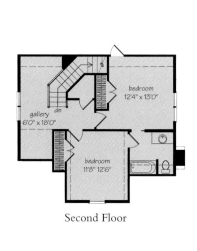

Second Floor

2,051 square feet

West Bay Landing

3 *Bedrooms* | 3 *Full Baths* | 1 *Half Bath*

PLAN #HPK3400123

Designed by Lake | Flato Architects Inc. for St. Joe Land Company

First Floor: 1,197 sq. ft.

Second Floor: 854 sq. ft.

Total: 2,051 sq. ft.

Width: 32' - 0"

Depth: 98' - 2"

Foundation: Pier (same as Piling)

1-800-850-1491
eplans.com

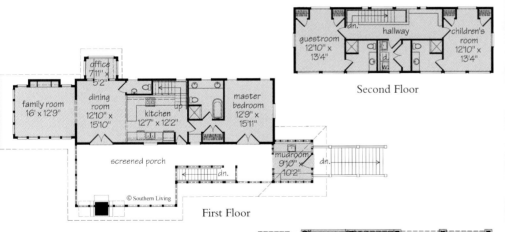

Second Floor

guestroom 12'10" x 13'4"

hallway

children's room 12'10" x 13'4"

dn.

family room 16' x 12'9"

office 7'11" x 5'2"

dining room 12'10" x 15'10"

kitchen 12'7" x 12'2"

up

master bedroom 12'9" x 15'11"

screened porch

mudroom 9'10" x 10'2"

dn.

dn.

© Southern Living

First Floor

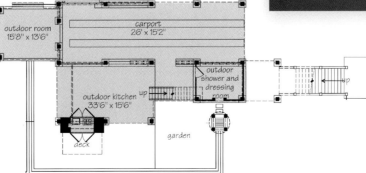

outdoor room 15'8" x 13'6"

carport 26' x 15'2"

outdoor shower and dressing room

outdoor kitchen 33'6" x 15'6"

up

up

garden

deck

Barrier Island Escape

ARCHITECTURAL RENDERING: MUIR STEWART

PLAN #HPK3400040

Designed by Allison-Ramsey Architects, Inc. for Coastal Living Magazine

2 Bedrooms   **2 Full Baths**

First Floor: 1,463 sq. ft.

Second Floor: 597 sq. ft.

Total: 2,060 sq. ft.

Width: 43' - 0"

Depth: 40' - 0"

Foundation: Pier (same as Piling)

1-800-850-1491
eplans.com

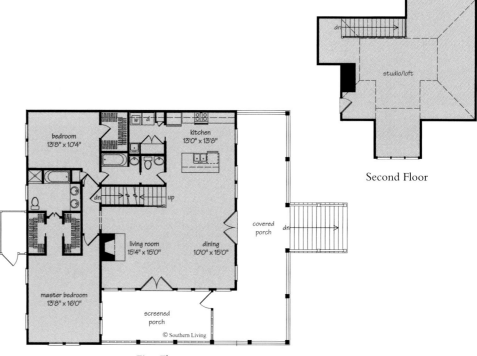

Second Floor

First Floor

Ogletree Lane

4 Bedrooms | 3 Full Baths

PLAN #HPK3400068

Designed by Moser Design Group

First Floor: 1,667 sq. ft.

Second Floor: 399 sq. ft.

Total: 2,066 sq. ft.

Width: 42' - 2"

Depth: 62' - 1"

Foundation: Crawlspace

1-800-850-1491
eplans.com

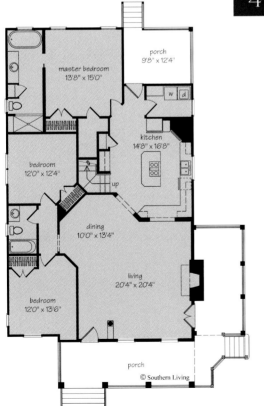

porch
9'8" x 12'4"

master bedroom
13'8" x 15'0"

w d

kitchen
14'8" x 16'8"

bedroom
12'0" x 12'4"

up

dining
10'0" x 13'4"

living
20'4" x 20'4"

bedroom
12'0" x 13'6"

porch

© Southern Living

First Floor

bedroom
12'8" x 13'8"

dn

gallery
7'4" x 10'8"

Second Floor

Cotton Hill Cottage

PLAN #HPK3400025

Designed by Bryan & Contreras, LLC

First Floor: 1,161 sq. ft.

Second Floor: 922 sq. ft.

Total: 2,083 sq. ft.

Width: 36' - 4"

Depth: 46' - 6"

Foundation: Crawlspace

1-800-850-1491
eplans.com

2 or 3 Bedrooms | *3 Full Baths*

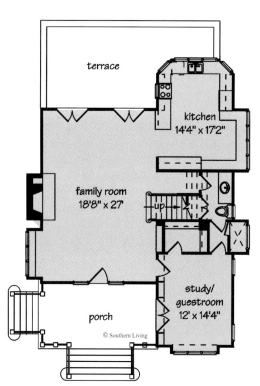

terrace

kitchen
14'4" x 17'2"

family room
18'8" x 27

up

study/
guestroom
12' x 14'4"

porch

© Southern Living

First Floor

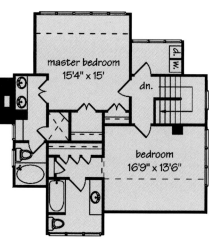

master bedroom
15'4" x 15'

dn.

bedroom
16'9" x 13'6"

Second Floor

Couples Cottage

2,090 square feet

ARCHITECTURAL RENDERING: MUIR STEWART

| 2 *Bedrooms* | 2 *Full Baths* | 1 *Half Bath* |

PLAN #HPK3400042

Designed by Moser Design Group for Coastal Living Magazine

First Floor: 1,162 sq. ft.

Second Floor: 928 sq. ft.

Total: 2,090 sq. ft.

Width: 42' – 10"

Depth: 55' – 10"

Foundation: Crawlspace

1-800-850-1491
eplans.com

First Floor

Second Floor

Chinaberry

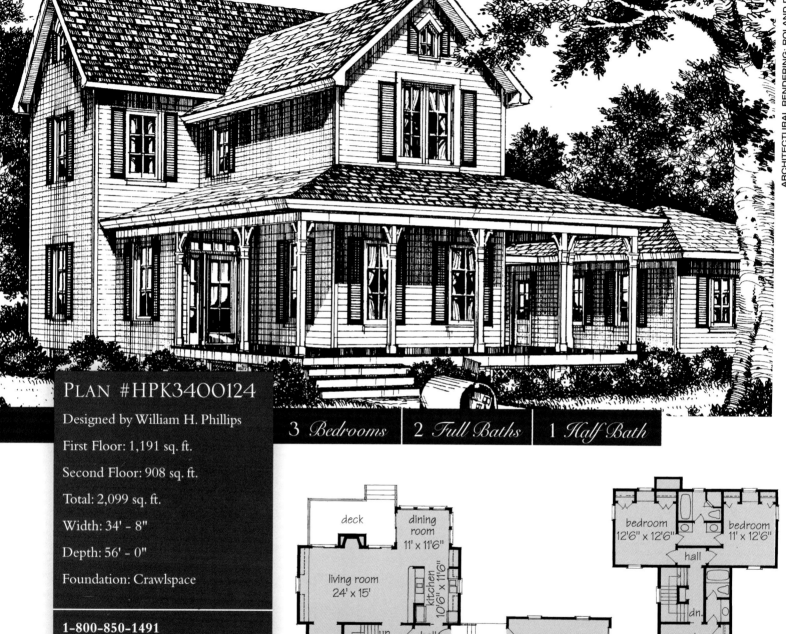

ARCHITECTURAL RENDERING: ROLAND DAVIS

PLAN #HPK3400124

Designed by William H. Phillips

First Floor: 1,191 sq. ft.

Second Floor: 908 sq. ft.

Total: 2,099 sq. ft.

Width: 34' - 8"

Depth: 56' - 0"

Foundation: Crawlspace

1-800-850-1491
eplans.com

3 *Bedrooms* | 2 *Full Baths* | 1 *Half Bath*

deck

dining room
11' x 11'6"

living room
24' x 15'

kitchen
10'6" x 11'6"

up

hall

foyer

w. d.

garage
21' x 24'

© Southern Living

library/ study
14'6" x 11'

porch

First Floor

bedroom
12'6" x 12'6"

bedroom
11' x 12'6"

hall

dn.

master bedroom
12' x 11'

Second Floor

Williams Bluff

MILES MELTON

3 Bedrooms | **2 Full Baths** | **1 Half Bath**

PLAN #HPK3400023

Designed by Moser Design Group

First Floor: 1,534 sq. ft.

Second Floor: 610 sq. ft.

Total: 2,144 sq. ft.

Width: 39' - 11"

Depth: 66' - 5"

Foundation: Crawlspace

1-800-850-1491
eplans.com

First Floor

Second Floor

Lowcountry Cottage

ARCHITECTURAL RENDERING: RICHARD CHENOWETH

PLAN #HPK3400005

Designed by Moser Design Group
for Cottage Living Magazine

First Floor: 1,631 sq. ft.

Second Floor: 517 sq. ft.

Total: 2,148 sq. ft.

Width: 44' - 10"

Depth: 73' - 0"

Foundation: Crawlspace

1-800-850-1491
eplans.com

| 2 Bedrooms | 2 Full Baths | 1 Half Bath |

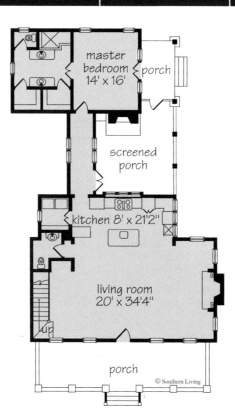

master bedroom 14' x 16'

porch

screened porch

kitchen 8' x 21'2"

living room 20' x 34'4"

porch

© Southern Living

First Floor

bedroom 13'8" x 20'

dn

Second Floor

Maple Hill

3 *Bedrooms* | 2 *Full Baths* | 1 *Half Bath*

PLAN #HPK3400026

Designed by Sullivan Design Company

First Floor: 1,635 sq. ft.

Second Floor: 534 sq. ft.

Total: 2,169 sq. ft.

Bonus Space: 241 sq. ft.

Width: 56' - 8"

Depth: 62' - 10"

Foundation: Crawlspace

1-800-850-1491
eplans.com

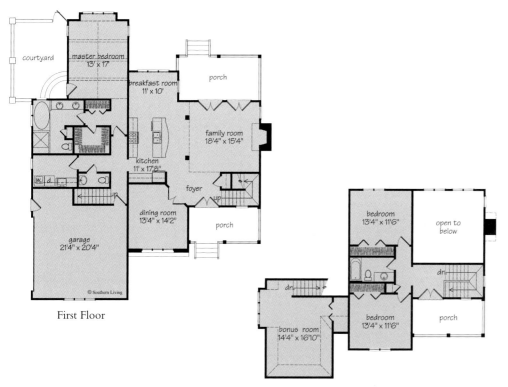

First Floor

Second Floor

2,188 square feet

Inlet Retreat

PLAN #HPK3400049

Designed by Allison-Ramsey Architects, Inc. for Coastal Living Magazine

First Floor: 1,604 sq. ft.

Second Floor: 584 sq. ft.

Total: 2,188 sq. ft.

Width: 52' - 0"

Depth: 42' - 0"

Foundation: Pier (same as Piling)

1-800-850-1491
eplans.com

3 *Bedrooms* | 3 *Full Baths*

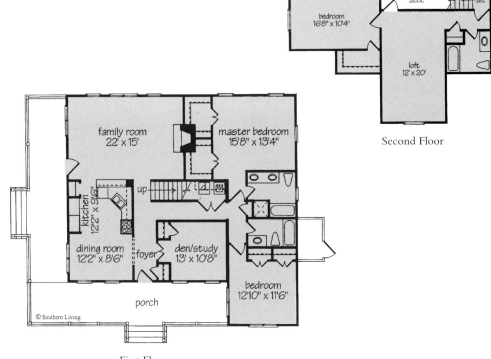

Second Floor

First Floor

Summer Cottage

2,195 square feet

3 *Bedrooms*   3 *Full Baths*

PLAN #HPK3400072

Designed by George Graves, AIA for Coastal Living Magazine

First Floor: 1,226 sq. ft.

Second Floor: 969 sq. ft.

Total: 2,195 sq. ft.

Width: 31' - 6"

Depth: 58' - 6"

Foundation: Crawlspace

1-800-850-1491
eplans.com

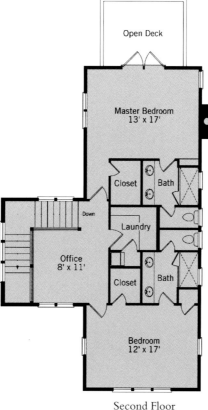

Screened Porch

© Southern Living

Living Room
16' x 17'

Dining Room
15'6" x 10'

Kitchen
11' x 12'

Foyer

Bath

Up

Entry
Porch

Bedroom
12' x 17'

First Floor

Open Deck

Master Bedroom
13' x 17'

Closet   Bath

Down

Laundry

Office
8' x 11'

Closet   Bath

Bedroom
12' x 17'

Second Floor

Carlisle House

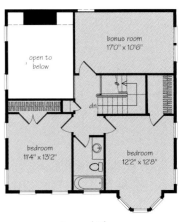

ARCHITECTURAL RENDERING: MILES MELTON

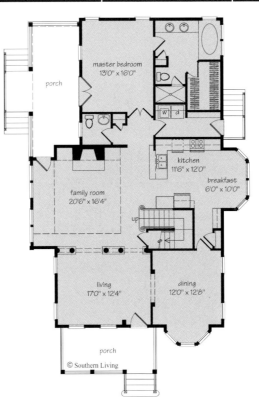

MILES MELTON

PLAN #HPK3400067

Designed by Moser Design Group

First Floor: 1,658 sq. ft.

Second Floor: 538 sq. ft.

Total: 2,196 sq. ft.

Bonus Space: 208 sq. ft.

Width: 37' - 0"

Depth: 61' - 8"

Foundation: Crawlspace

1-800-850-1491
eplans.com

3 Bedrooms | *2 Full Baths* | *1 Half Bath*

porch

master bedroom
13'0" x 16'0"

w d

kitchen
11'6" x 12'0"

breakfast
6'0" x 10'0"

family room
20'6" x 16'4"

up

living
17'0" x 12'4"

dining
12'0" x 12'8"

porch

© Southern Living

First Floor

open to below

bonus room
17'0" x 10'6"

dn

bedroom
11'4" x 13'2"

bedroom
12'2" x 12'8"

Second Floor

Aiken Ridge

ARCHITECTURAL RENDERING: MILES MELTON

3 *Bedrooms* | **3** *Full Baths* | **1** *Half Bath*

PLAN #HPK3400006

Designed by Moser Design Group

First Floor: 1,580 sq. ft.

Second Floor: 622 sq. ft.

Total: 2,202 sq. ft.

Width: 40' - 1"

Depth: 60' - 0"

Foundation: Crawlspace

1-800-850-1491
eplans.com

First Floor

Second Floor

New Rustic Oaks

PLAN #HPK3400038

Designed by John Tee, Architect

Square Footage: 2,208

Width: 80' - 0"

Depth: 47' - 6"

Foundation: Crawlspace

1-800-850-1491
eplans.com

3 *Bedrooms* | 2 *Full Baths* | 1 *Half Bath*

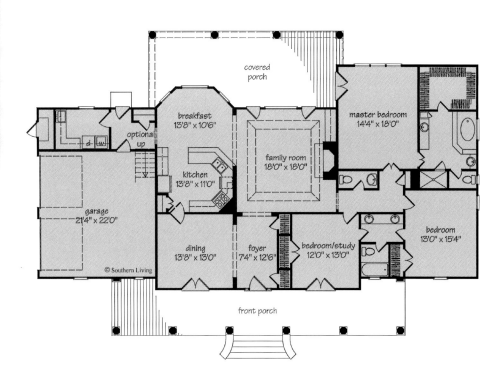

covered porch

breakfast
13'8" x 10'6"

master bedroom
14'4" x 18'0"

optional up

kitchen
13'8" x 11'0"

family room
18'0" x 18'0"

garage
21'4" x 22'0"

bedroom
13'0" x 15'4"

dining
13'8" x 13'0"

foyer
7'4" x 12'6"

bedroom/study
12'0" x 13'0"

© Southern Living

front porch

Bradley House

,218 square feet

| 3 *Bedrooms* | 3 *Full Baths* | 1 *Half Bath* |

PLAN #HPK3400007

Designed by Moser Design Group

First Floor: 1,412 sq. ft.

Second Floor: 806 sq. ft.

Total: 2,218 sq. ft.

Width: 43' – 6"

Depth: 51' – 11"

Foundation: Crawlspace

1-800-850-1491
eplans.com

First Floor

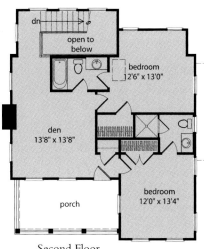

Second Floor

Mad Trapper

PLAN #HPK3400102

Designed by John Tee, Architect
for Reynolds Landing

4 Bedrooms | **3 Full Baths** | **1 Half Bath**

Main Level: 1,208 sq. ft.

Lower Level: 1,051 sq. ft.

Total: 2,259 sq. ft.

Width: 44' - 0"

Depth: 46' - 0"

Foundation: Finished Walkout
Basement

1-800-850-1491
eplans.com

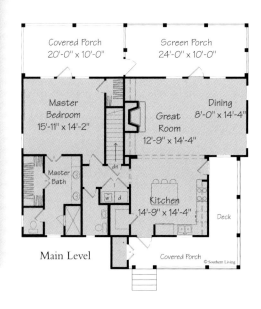

Main Level

Covered Porch
20'-0" x 10'-0"

Screen Porch
24'-0" x 10'-0"

Master
Bedroom
15'-11" x 14'-2"

Great
Room
12'-9" x 14'-4"

Dining
8'-0" x 14'-4"

Master
Bath

Kitchen
14'-9" x 14'-4"

Deck

Covered Porch
© Southern Living

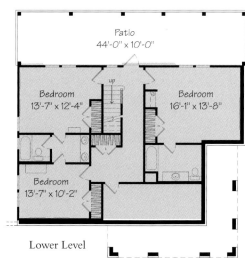

Lower Level

Patio
44'-0" x 10'-0"

Bedroom
13'-7" x 12'-4"

Bedroom
16'-1" x 13'-8"

Bedroom
13'-7" x 10'-2"

Spincaster Cottage

4 Bedrooms	3 Full Baths	1 Half Bath

PLAN #HPK3400103

Designed by John Tee, Architect for Reynolds Landing

Main Level: 1,208 sq. ft.

Lower Level: 1,051 sq. ft.

Total: 2,259 sq. ft.

Width: 44' - 0"

Depth: 46' - 0"

Foundation: Finished Walkout Basement

1-800-850-1491
eplans.com

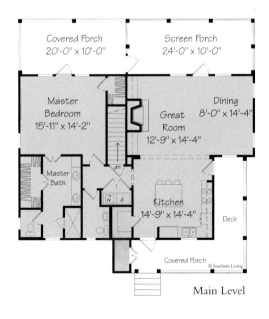

Covered Porch 20'-0" x 10'-0"

Screen Porch 24'-0" x 10'-0"

Master Bedroom 15'-11" x 14'-2"

Great Room 12'-9" x 14'-4"

Dining 8'-0" x 14'-4"

Master Bath

Kitchen 14'-9" x 14'-4"

Deck

Covered Porch

© Southern Living

Main Level

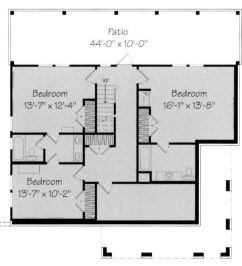

Patio 44'-0" x 10'-0"

Bedroom 13'-7" x 12'-4"

Bedroom 16'-1" x 13'-8"

Bedroom 13'-7" x 10'-2"

Lower Level

Harborside Hideaway

MUIR STEWART

PLAN #HPK3400117

Designed by Looney Ricks Kiss Architects, Inc. for Coastal Living Magazine

First Floor: 1,278 sq. ft.

Second Floor: 1,010 sq. ft.

Total: 2,288 sq. ft.

Width: 56' - 3"

Depth: 40' - 9"

Foundation: Pier (same as Piling)

1-800-850-1491
eplans.com

4 *Bedrooms* | 3 *Full Baths*

THIS DESIGN IS IDEAL FOR

waterfront lots, where its deep, wraparound porch and panoramic fenestrations can take in views of the sun setting over the horizon. The layout is casual and interactive, with a large island kitchen providing for everyday dining and simple entertaining. Very ample storage areas are found throughout the home, as well as a full-sized laundry. Bedrooms feel private; the master suite accesses a private covered balcony. The elevator to the lower level is a thoughtful accommodation. ✺

ARCHITECTURAL RENDERING: MUIR STEWART

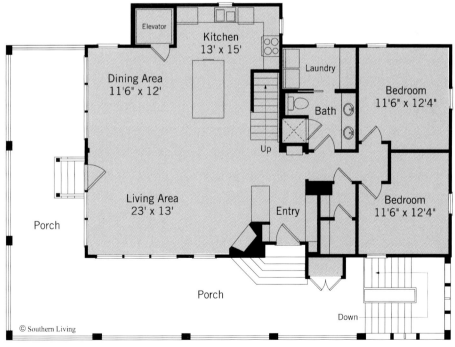

Second Floor

Sitting Area
9'6" x 9'

Down

Closet

Closet

Closet

Balcony
7' x 12'

Master Bedroom
14' x 14'

Bath

Bath

Bunk Room
11'4" x 17'6"

Closet

First Floor

Elevator

Kitchen
13' x 15'

Laundry

Dining Area
11'6" x 12'

Bath

Bedroom
11'6" x 12'4"

Living Area
23' x 13'

Up

Entry

Bedroom
11'6" x 12'4"

Porch

Porch

Down

© Southern Living

Angel Oak Point

ARCHITECTURAL RENDERING: MILES MELTON

PLAN #HPK3400069

Designed by Moser Design Group

First Floor: 1,462 sq. ft.

Second Floor: 837 sq. ft.

Total: 2,299 sq. ft.

Width: 32' - 4"

Depth: 70' - 8"

Foundation: Crawlspace

1-800-850-1491
eplans.com

3 *Bedrooms* | 3 *Full Baths* | 1 *Half Bath*

Second Floor

First Floor

River View Cottage

| 3 *Bedrooms* | 2 *Full Baths* | 1 *Half Bath* |

PLAN #HPK3400047

Designed by Looney Ricks Kiss Architects, Inc.

First Floor: 1,234 sq. ft.

Second Floor: 1,081 sq. ft.

Total: 2,315 sq. ft.

Width: 34' – 0"

Depth: 95' – 0"

Foundation: Crawlspace

1-800-850-1491
eplans.com

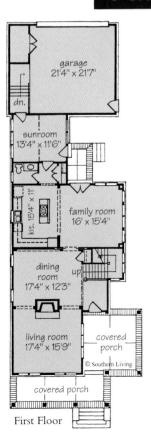

garage
21'4" x 21'7"

dn.

sunroom
13'4" x 11'6"

kit. 15'4" x 11'

family room
16' x 15'4"

dining room
17'4" x 12'3"

up

living room
17'4" x 15'9"

covered porch

© Southern Living

covered porch

First Floor

bedroom
11' x 14'4"

bedroom
10' x 13'

W/D

dn.

master bedroom
17'4" x 15'9"

covered porch

Second Floor

Wildmere Cottage

PLAN #HPK3400065

Designed by Moser Design Group
for Cottage Living Magazine

First Floor: 1,435 sq. ft.

Second Floor: 910 sq. ft.

Total: 2,345 sq. ft.

Width: 44' - 0"

Depth: 66' - 7"

Foundation: Crawlspace

1-800-850-1491
eplans.com

| 3 Bedrooms | 3 Full Baths | 1 Half Bath |

Second Floor

First Floor

© Southern Living

Franklin House

ARCHITECTURAL RENDERING: MILES MELLIN

3 Bedrooms | **3 Full Baths** | **1 Half Bath**

PLAN #HPK3400125

Designed by Mouzon Design

First Floor: 1,704 sq. ft.

Second Floor: 648 sq. ft.

Total: 2,352 sq. ft.

Width: 45' - 0"

Depth: 91' - 0"

Foundation: Crawlspace

1-800-850-1491
eplans.com

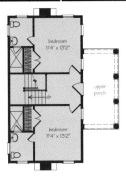

Second Floor

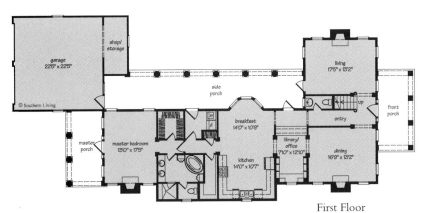

First Floor

Winnsboro Heights

PLAN #HPK3400131

Designed by Moser Design Group

First Floor: 1,462 sq. ft.

Second Floor: 893 sq. ft.

Total: 2,355 sq. ft.

Width: 41' - 4"

Depth: 59' - 1"

Foundation: Crawlspace

1-800-850-1491
eplans.com

4 Bedrooms | *2 Full Baths* | *1 Half Bath*

First Floor

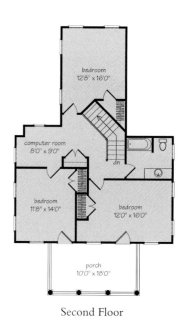

Second Floor

Tabor Lane

MILES MELTON

3 *Bedrooms* | **3** *Full Baths* | **1** *Half Bath*

PLAN #HPK3400132

Designed by Moser Design Group

First Floor: 1,421 sq. ft.

Second Floor: 939 sq. ft.

Total: 2,360 sq. ft.

Width: 42' - 0"

Depth: 58' - 6"

Foundation: Crawlspace

1-800-850-1491
eplans.com

master bedroom
15'6" x 14'0"

porch

screened
porch
12'0" x 13'0"

kitchen
17'0" x 11'0"

up

living room
22'0" x 19'0"

dining
17'0" x 10'0"

porch

© Southern Living

First Floor

dn

gallery

bedroom
14'2" x 13'5"

study
10'0" x 9'4"

bedroom
14'2" x 13'5"

porch

Second Floor

Rambert Place

PLAN #HPK3400128

Designed by Moser Design Group

First Floor: 1,565 sq. ft.

Second Floor: 799 sq. ft.

Total: 2,364 sq. ft.

Width: 36' - 2"

Depth: 59' - 8"

Foundation: Crawlspace

1-800-850-1491
eplans.com

4 *Bedrooms* | 3 *Full Baths* | 1 *Half Bath*

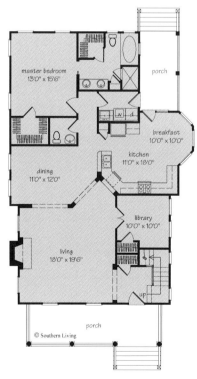

First Floor

© Southern Living

Second Floor

2007 Cottage Living Idea Home

ARCHITECTURAL RENDERING: RICHARD CHENOWETH

| 3 *Bedrooms* | 2 *Full Baths* | 1 *Half Bath* |

PLAN #HPK3400118

Designed by Moser Design Group
for Cottage Living Magazine

First Floor: 1,192 sq. ft.

Second Floor: 1,178 sq. ft.

Total: 2,370 sq. ft.

Width: 24' - 0"

Depth: 77' - 8"

Foundation: Crawlspace

**1-800-850-1491
eplans.com**

First Floor

Second Floor

Southern Living Style

Mabry Cottage

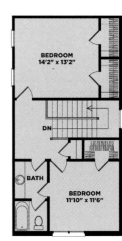

PLAN #HPK3400082

Designed by Looney Ricks Kiss Architects, Inc. for Cottage Living Magazine

3 *Bedrooms* | **2** *Full Baths* | **1** *Half Bath*

First Floor: 1,774 sq. ft.

Second Floor: 598 sq. ft.

Total: 2,372 sq. ft.

Width: 37' - 6"

Depth: 72' - 7"

Foundation: Slab

1-800-850-1491
eplans.com

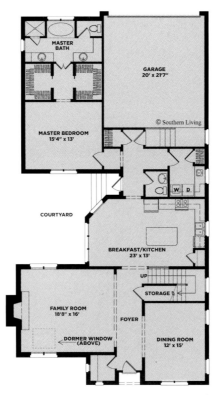

MASTER BATH

GARAGE
20' x 21'7"

© Southern Living

MASTER BEDROOM
15'4" x 13'

COURTYARD

W D

BREAKFAST/KITCHEN
23' x 13'

UP

STORAGE

FAMILY ROOM
18'8" x 16'

FOYER

DORMER WINDOW
(ABOVE)

DINING ROOM
12' x 15'

First Floor

BEDROOM
14'2" x 13'2"

DN

BATH

BEDROOM
11'10" x 11'6"

Second Floor

Peachtree Cottage

2,390 square feet

3 *Bedrooms* | 2 *Full Baths* | 1 *Half Bath*

PLAN #HPK3400054

Designed by John Tee, Architect

Square Footage: 2,390

Width: 81' - 0"

Depth: 55' - 0"

Foundation: Crawlspace, Unfinished Basement

1-800-850-1491
eplans.com

garage
23'6" x 26'

screened porch

deck

breakfast bay
13'6" x 10'

family room
21' x 15'6"

master bedroom
16'6" x 15'

up

© Southern Living

kitchen
13'6" x 14'6"

dn.

w. d.

dining room
13' x 14'

foyer

bedroom or living/study
14'6" x 13'

bedroom
11'6" x 15'

porch

Lakeside Cottage

PLAN #HPK3400001

Designed by William H. Phillips

Square Footage: 2,400

Bonus Space: 192 sq. ft.

Width: 76' – 3"

Depth: 65' – 9"

Foundation: Crawlspace

1-800-850-1491
eplans.com

3 *Bedrooms* | 2 *Full Baths* | 1 *Half Bath*

© Southern Living

Pennington Point

2,401 square feet

MILES MELTON

3 Bedrooms | **2** Full Baths | **1** Half Bath

PLAN #HPK3400127

Designed by Moser Design Group

First Floor: 1,764 sq. ft.

Second Floor: 637 sq. ft.

Total: 2,401 sq. ft.

Width: 48' – 9"

Depth: 78' – 4"

Foundation: Crawlspace

1-800-850-1491
eplans.com

gallery
dn

bedroom
11'10" x 14'1"

bedroom
15'8" x 13'3"

Second Floor

master bedroom
14'0" x 17'0"

up

w

kitchen
18'0" x 14'0"

dining
11'2" x 16'0"

porch

great room
18'0" x 18'8"

screen
porch

library
15'4" x 11'2"

© Southern Living

First Floor

New Oxford

PLAN #HPK3400002

Designed by John Tee, Architect

Square Footage: 2,404

Width: 70' - 0"

Depth: 63' - 0"

Foundation: Unfinished Basement

1-800-850-1491
eplans.com

3 *Bedrooms* | 2 *Full Baths* | 1 *Half Bath*

Glenview Cottage

3 *Bedrooms* | **2** *Full Baths* | **1** *Half Bath*

PLAN #HPK3400044

Designed by Moser Design Group for Cottage Living Magazine

First Floor: 1,712 sq. ft.

Second Floor: 702 sq. ft.

Total: 2,414 sq. ft.

Width: 45' – 0"

Depth: 67' – 0"

Foundation: Crawlspace

1-800-850-1491
eplans.com

First Floor

- SCREENED PORCH 11'4"x13'8"
- UTILITY
- PANTRY
- PWDR
- UP
- DINING ROOM 11'8"x14'
- MASTER BATH
- WIC
- WIC
- MASTER BEDROOM 14'x17'
- KITCHEN 14'x15'
- LIVING ROOM 17'6"x18'
- DEN 12'x13'8"
- PORCH 9'6" DEEP

Second Floor

- OPEN TO BELOW
- DN
- BATH
- LANDING 11'x16'
- BEDROOM #2 13'6"x14'8"
- STORAGE
- BEDROOM #3 11'8"x13'8"

Southern Living Style

Downing Cottage

PLAN #HPK3400099

Designed by Caldwell-Cline Architects and Designers for Cottage Living Magazine

First Floor: 1,538 sq. ft.

Second Floor: 879 sq. ft.

Total: 2,417 sq. ft.

Width: 55' - 2"

Depth: 50' - 8"

Foundation: Daylight Basement

1-800-850-1491
eplans.com

4 *Bedrooms* | 3 *Full Baths*

First Floor

Second Floor

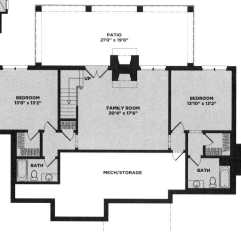

Southern Living *Style*

Pleasant Hill Cottage

| 3 *Bedrooms* | 2 *Full Baths* | 1 *Half Bath* |

PLAN #HPK3400076

Designed by Bryan & Contreras, LLC

First Floor: 1,814 sq. ft.

Second Floor: 607 sq. ft.

Total: 2,421 sq. ft.

Width: 61' – 2"

Depth: 53' – 6"

Foundation: Unfinished Basement

1-800-850-1491
eplans.com

First Floor

Second Floor

Westbury Park

PLAN #HPK3400004

Designed by Moser Design Group

First Floor: 1,905 sq. ft.

Second Floor: 552 sq. ft.

Total: 2,457 sq. ft.

Width: 66' - 2"

Depth: 52' - 8"

Foundation: Crawlspace

1-800-850-1491
eplans.com

3 Bedrooms | 2 Full Baths | 1 Half Bath

First Floor

Second Floor

St. Helena House

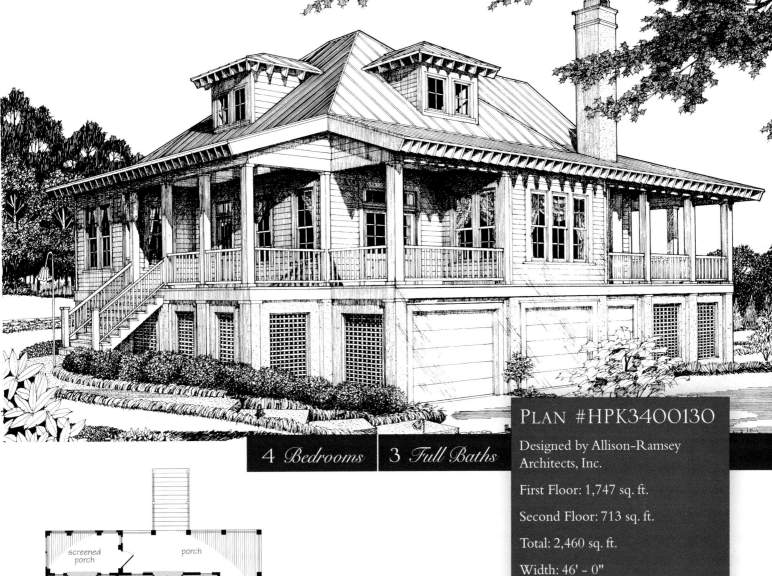

4 Bedrooms | **3 Full Baths**

PLAN #HPK3400130

Designed by Allison-Ramsey Architects, Inc.

First Floor: 1,747 sq. ft.

Second Floor: 713 sq. ft.

Total: 2,460 sq. ft.

Width: 46' - 0"

Depth: 60' - 0"

Foundation: Pier (same as Piling)

1-800-850-1491
eplans.com

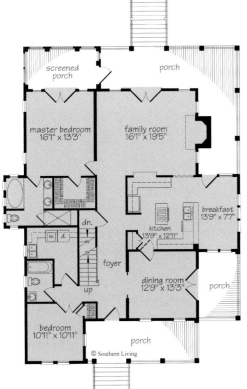

First Floor

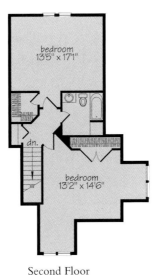

Second Floor

Stonebridge Cottage

ARCHITECTURAL RENDERING: LOIS WATSON

PLAN #HPK3400015

Designed by Sullivan Design Company

First Floor: 1,696 sq. ft.

Second Floor: 788 sq. ft.

Total: 2,484 sq. ft.

Bonus Space: 397 sq. ft.

Width: 59' - 8"

Depth: 76' - 2"

Foundation: Crawlspace

1-800-850-1491
eplans.com

4 *Bedrooms* | 3 *Full Baths* | 1 *Half Bath*

Second Floor

First Floor

Our Gulf Coast Cottage

ARCHITECTURAL RENDERING: ROLAND DAVIS

3 *Bedrooms* | 2 *Full Baths* | 1 *Half Bath*

PLAN #HPK3400045

Designed by William H. Phillips

Square Footage: 2,496

Width: 50' - 0"

Depth: 74' - 0"

Foundation: Crawlspace

1-800-850-1491
eplans.com

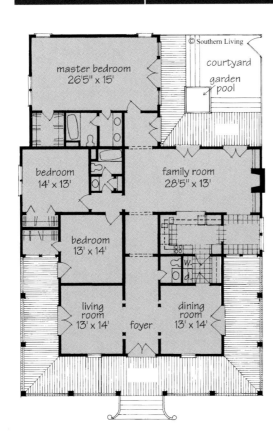

© Southern Living

master bedroom
26'5" x 15'

courtyard

garden
pool

bedroom
14' x 13'

family room
28'5" x 13'

bedroom
13' x 14'

living
room
13' x 14'

foyer

dining
room
13' x 14'

w
d

Cottage of the Year

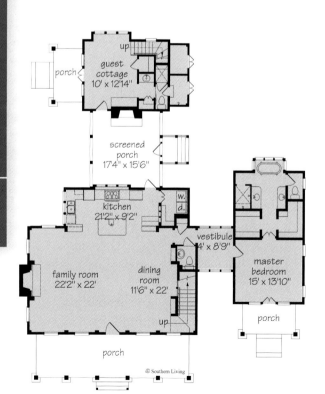

ARCHITECTURAL RENDERING: MUIR STEWART

PLAN #HPK3400011

Designed by Moser Design Group for Coastal Living Magazine

First Floor: 2,028 sq. ft.

Second Floor: 584 sq. ft.

Total: 2,612 sq. ft.

Width: 63' – 0"

Depth: 76' – 0"

Foundation: Pier (same as Piling)

1-800-850-1491
eplans.com

4 Bedrooms | *3 Full Baths* | *1 Half Bath*

porch

guest cottage
10' x 12'14"

screened
porch
17'4" x 15'6"

kitchen
21'2" x 9'2"

w.
d.

family room
22'2" x 22'

dining
room
11'6" x 22'

vestibule
14' x 8'9"

master
bedroom
15' x 13'10"

porch

up

porch

© Southern Living

First Floor

open to
below

guest
cottage
loft

dn.

storage

bedroom
13'2" x 12'

mech. room

bedroom
15' x 12'

open
to
below

storage

Second Floor

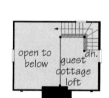

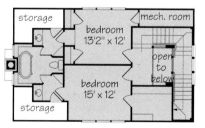

Camden Cottage

68

| 4 *Bedrooms* | 3 *Full Baths* | 1 *Half Bath* |

PLAN #HPK3400133

Designed by Mouzon Design for Cottage Living Magazine

First Floor: 1,508 sq. ft.

Second Floor: 1,022 sq. ft.

Total: 2,530 sq. ft.

Width: 37' – 0"

Depth: 91' – 0"

Foundation: Crawlspace, Slab

1-800-850-1491
eplans.com

garage
21'9" x 21'9"

© Southern Living

master
bedroom
12'9" x 13'4"

porch

breakfast
room
9'6" x
8'2"

keeping
room
14'6" x
14'2"

11'6"
x
8'2"
kitchen

office
7'10" x
9'6"

family room/dining room
15'4" x 23'

porch

First Floor

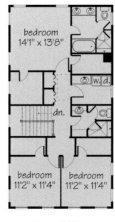

bedroom
14'1" x 13'8"

w. d.

dn.

bedroom
11'2" x 11'4"

bedroom
11'2" x 11'4"

Second Floor

Pine Hill Cottage

PLAN #HPK3400077

Designed by Bryan &
Contreras, LLC

First Floor: 1,938 sq. ft.

Second Floor: 651 sq. ft.

Total: 2,589 sq. ft.

Width: 53' - 0"

Depth: 52' - 6"

Foundation: Unfinished Basement

1-800-850-1491
eplans.com

4 *Bedrooms* | 3 *Full Baths*

First Floor

Second Floor

3 *Bedrooms* | 4 *Full Baths*

PLAN #HPK3400134

Designed by Bryan & Contreras, LLC

First Floor: 1,389 sq. ft.

Second Floor: 1,213 sq. ft.

Total: 2,602 sq. ft.

Width: 47' - 4"

Depth: 46' - 0"

Foundation: Crawlspace

1-800-850-1491
eplans.com

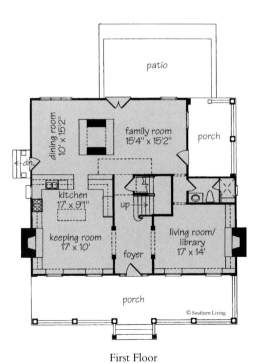

First Floor

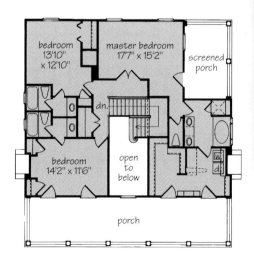

Second Floor

ARCHITECTURAL RENDERING: MUIR STEWART

PLAN #HPK3400084

Designed by Mel Snyder, Domain Design for Coastal Living Magazine

| 3 Bedrooms | 2 Full Baths | 2 Half Baths |

First Floor: 870 sq. ft.

Second Floor: 1,170 sq. ft.

Third Floor: 582 sq. ft.

Total: 2,622 sq. ft.

Width: 30' - 0"

Depth: 55' - 0"

Foundation: Pier (same as Piling)

1-800-850-1491
eplans.com

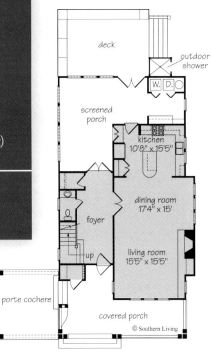

First Floor

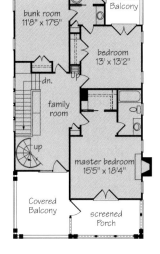

Second Floor

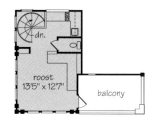

Third Floor

Poplar Creek Cottage

2,628 square feet

ARCHITECTURAL RENDERING: LOIS WATSON

| 3 *Bedrooms* | 2 *Full Baths* | 1 *Half Bath* |

PLAN #HPK3400053

Designed by Bryan & Contreras, LLC

First Floor: 2,026 sq. ft.

Second Floor: 602 sq. ft.

Total: 2,628 sq. ft.

Width: 45' – 6"

Depth: 81' – 10"

Foundation: Unfinished Basement

1-800-850-1491
eplans.com

First Floor

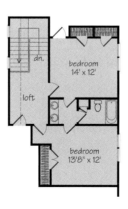

Second Floor

ARCHITECTURAL RENDERING: MILES MELTON

PLAN #HPK3400052

Designed by Mouzon Design

First Floor: 1,978 sq. ft.

Second Floor: 661 sq. ft.

Total: 2,639 sq. ft.

Width: 81' - 4"

Depth: 64' - 0"

Foundation: Unfinished Basement

1-800-850-1491
eplans.com

3 Bedrooms | *2 Full Baths* | *1 Half Bath*

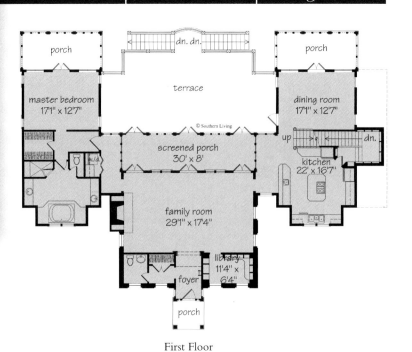

First Floor

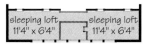

Second Floor

Alta Vista

3 *Bedrooms* | 2 *Full Baths* | 1 *Half Bath*

PLAN #HPK3400059

Designed by Mouzon Design
for Biltmore Estate

First Floor: 1,823 sq. ft.

Second Floor: 822 sq. ft.

Total: 2,645 sq. ft.

Width: 71' – 0"

Depth: 75' – 1"

Foundation: Crawlspace

1-800-850-1491
eplans.com

First Floor

- master bedroom 15'1" x 15'1"
- library/nursery 13'1" x 9'5"
- porch
- optional b'fast room 7'6" x 9'1"
- garage 22'5" x 22'5"
- © Southern Living
- up
- friends' entry
- kitchen 11'7" x 16'3"
- family room 23'8" x 21'7"
- w. d.
- dining room 15'1" x 11'10"
- porch

Second Floor

- bedroom 14'1" x 14'1"
- bedroom 14'1" x 14'1"
- sitting room 17'1" x 9'9"
- dn.

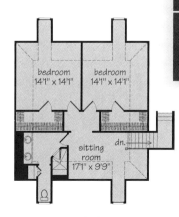

BILTMORE™
For Your Home

Turnball Park

PLAN #HPK3400066

Designed by Moser Design Group

First Floor: 1,537 sq. ft.

Second Floor: 1,123 sq. ft.

Total: 2,660 sq. ft.

Width: 40' - 0"

Depth: 70' - 0"

Foundation: Crawlspace

1-800-850-1491
eplans.com

| 3 Bedrooms | 2 Full Baths | 1 Half Bath |

First Floor

Second Floor

2,673 square feet

Elderberry Place

3 or 4 Bedrooms | 3 Full Baths

PLAN #HPK3400039

Designed by Allison–Ramsey Architects, Inc.

First Floor: 1,933 sq. ft.

Second Floor: 740 sq. ft.

Total: 2,673 sq. ft.

Width: 44' - 0"

Depth: 61' - 0"

Foundation: Pier

1-800-850-1491
eplans.com

First Floor

porch

breakfast
14'0" x 10'8"

screen porch

© Southern Living

kitchen
14'0" x 14'0"

dining
12'8" x 13'6"

great room
16'0" x 19'6"

porch

foyer

up

den - bedroom
12'0" x 12'10"

master bedroom
16'0" x 13'4"

sunroom
7'8" x 12'6"

Second Floor

bedroom
15'4" x 10'0"

bedroom
10'0" x 16'0"

dn

Grissom Trail

PLAN #HPK3400135

Designed by Moser Design Group

First Floor: 1,554 sq. ft.

Second Floor: 1,123 sq. ft.

Total: 2,677 sq. ft.

Width: 39' – 4"

Depth: 67' – 0"

Foundation: Crawlspace

1-800-850-1491
eplans.com

4 *Bedrooms* | 3 *Full Baths* | 1 *Half Bath*

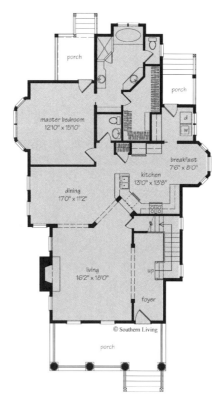

First Floor

Second Floor

© Southern Living

Bucktail Lodge

| 4 *Bedrooms* | 3 *Full Baths* | 1 *Half Bath* |

PLAN #HPK3400109

Designed by Caldwell-Cline Architects and Designers for Reynolds Landing

Main Level: 1,380 sq. ft.

Lower Level: 1,298 sq. ft.

Total: 2,678 sq. ft.

Width: 44' - 2"

Depth: 50' - 0"

Foundation: Finished Walkout Basement

1-800-850-1491
eplans.com

Main Level

Lower Level

Southern Living Style

Rattling Shad

PLAN #HPK3400110

Designed by Caldwell-Cline Architects and Designers for Reynolds Landing

Main Level: 1,380 sq. ft.

Lower Level: 1,298 sq. ft.

Total: 2,678 sq. ft.

Width: 44' - 2"

Depth: 50' - 0"

Foundation: Finished Basement

1-800-850-1491
eplans.com

4 *Bedrooms* | 3 *Full Baths* | 1 *Half Bath*

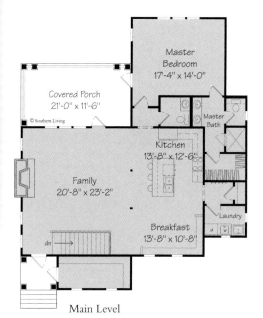

Main Level

Lower Level

Southern Living Style

Harborside Cottage

4 Bedrooms | **4 Full Baths**

PLAN #HPK3400073

Designed by Caldwell-Cline Architects and Designers for Coastal Living Magazine

First Floor: 1,600 sq. ft.

Second Floor: 1,089 sq. ft.

Total: 2,689 sq. ft.

Width: 47' - 8"

Depth: 54' - 8"

Foundation: Crawlspace

1-800-850-1491
eplans.com

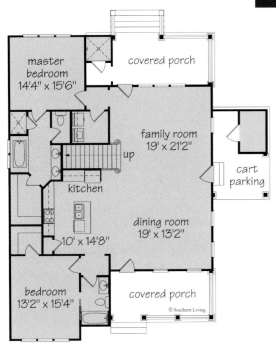

master bedroom 14'4" x 15'6"

covered porch

family room 19' x 21'2"

up

cart parking

kitchen

dining room 19' x 13'2"

10' x 14'8"

bedroom 13'2" x 15'4"

covered porch

© Southern Living

First Floor

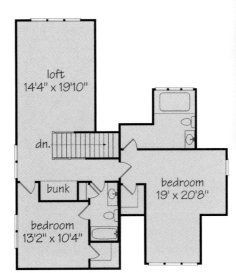

loft 14'4" x 19'10"

dn.

bunk

bedroom 13'2" x 10'4"

bedroom 19' x 20'8"

Second Floor

Southern Living *Style*

Hookset Hideaway

PLAN #HPK3400114

Design by Caldwell-Cline
Architects and Designers for
Reynolds Landing

Lower Level: 1,335 sq. ft.

Main Level: 1,360 sq. ft.

Total: 2,695 sq. ft.

Width: 44' - 6"

Depth: 52' - 0"

Foundation: Finished Basement

1-800-850-1491
...om

3 *Bedrooms* | 2 *Full Baths* | 1 *Half Bath*

CALDWELL-CLINE Architects and Designers have
made the best of this bungalow's efficient footprint, including a
wide-open layout that combines the kitchen, family room, and
dining area, as well as the front and rear porches. A small buffer zone, which includes a half bath and laundry, separates these
spaces from the master suite, situated at the rear of the plan.
When building on a hillside lot, additional living quarters can be
located in the walkout basement. Finish the space with a rec
room and additional bedrooms that can access the rear property
by way of the terrace. ❀

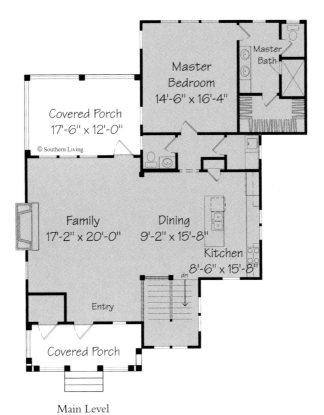

Covered Porch
17'-6" x 12'-0"

© Southern Living

Master
Bedroom
14'-6" x 16'-4"

Master
Bath

Family
17'-2" x 20'-0"

Dining
9'-2" x 15'-8"

Kitchen
8'-6" x 15'-8"

dn

Entry

Covered Porch

Main Level

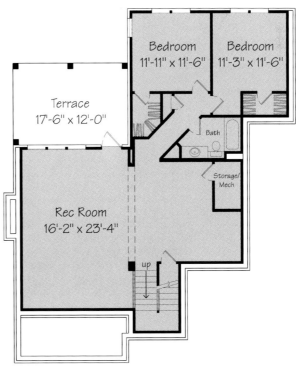

Terrace
17'-6" x 12'-0"

Bedroom
11'-11" x 11'-6"

Bedroom
11'-3" x 11'-6"

Bath

Storage/
Mech

Rec Room
16'-2" x 23'-4"

up

Lower Level

Sea Island House

PLAN #HPK3400051

Designed by Historical Concepts, LLC for Coastal Living Magazine

3 Bedrooms | **4 Full Baths**

First Floor: 1,584 sq. ft.

Second Floor: 1,154 sq. ft.

Total: 2,738 sq. ft.

Width: 65' - 0"

Depth: 44' - 0"

Foundation: Crawlspace

1-800-850-1491
eplans.com

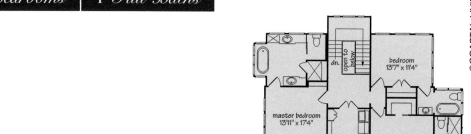

Second Floor

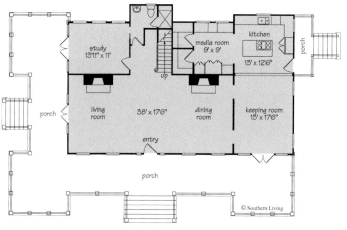

First Floor

McKenzie Cottage

2,750 square feet

3 or 4 *Bedrooms* | 4 *Full Baths*

PLAN #HPK3400003

Designed by Bryan & Contreras, LLC

First Floor: 1,930 sq. ft.

Second Floor: 820 sq. ft.

Total: 2,750 sq. ft.

Width: 60' – 8"

Depth: 46' – 6"

Foundation: Crawlspace

1-800-850-1491
eplans.com

Second Floor

First Floor

Bay Point Cottage

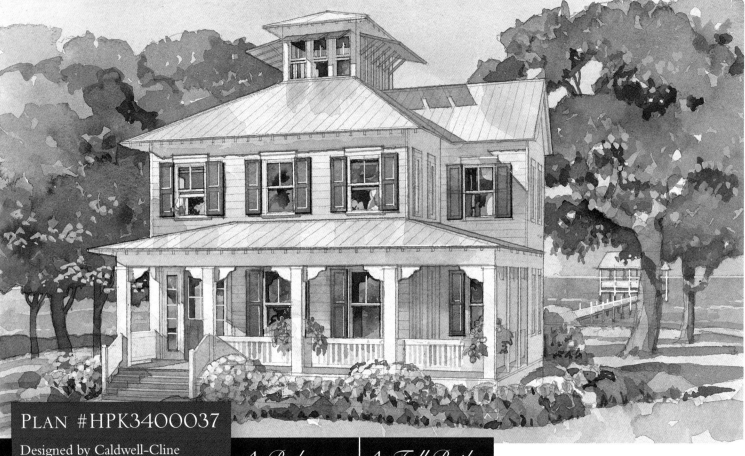

ARCHITECTURAL RENDERING: MUIR STEWART

PLAN #HPK3400037

Designed by Caldwell-Cline Architects and Designers for Coastal Living Magazine

First Floor: 1,424 sq. ft.

Second Floor: 1,376 sq. ft.

Third Floor: 124 sq. ft.

Total: 2,924 sq. ft.

Width: 35' - 0"

Depth: 58' - 6"

Foundation: Crawlspace

1-800-850-1491
eplans.com

4 *Bedrooms* | 4 *Full Baths*

family room 25'6" x 20'

dining area

kitchen 14'9" x 9'6"

foyer

bedroom/study 14'6" x 14'6"

d. w.

up

porch

© Southern Living

First Floor

master bedroom 16' x 19'

up

dn.

bedroom 13' x 13'6"

bedroom 13'6" x 13'6"

Second Floor

dn.

lookout 7'6" x 16'6"

Third Floor

Bedford Cottage

ARCHITECTURAL RENDERING: RICHARD CHENOWETH

3 *Bedrooms* | **2** *Full Baths* | **1** *Half Bath*

PLAN #HPK3400074

Designed by Looney Ricks Kiss Architects, Inc. for Cottage Living Magazine

First Floor: 1,589 sq. ft.

Second Floor: 1,362 sq. ft.

Total: 2,951 sq. ft.

Bonus Space: 490 sq. ft.

Width: 56' - 9"

Depth: 68' - 7"

Foundation: Crawlspace

1-800-850-1491
eplans.com

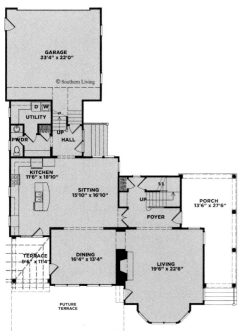

First Floor

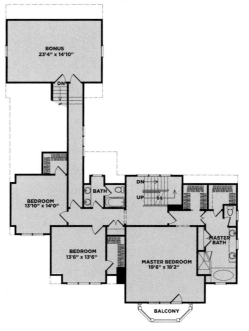

Second Floor

2,968 square feet

Hampstead Place

PLAN #HPK3400121

Designed by Geoff Chick and Associates, Inc.

First Floor: 2,273 sq. ft.

Second Floor: 695 sq. ft.

Total: 2,968 sq. ft.

Bonus Space: 389 sq. ft.

Width: 38' – 4"

Depth: 98' – 9"

Foundation: Pier (same as Piling)

1-800-850-1491
eplans.com

3 *Bedrooms* | 3 *Full Baths* | 1 *Half Bath*

First Floor

Second Floor

ARCHITECTURAL RENDERING: ROLAND DAVIS

| 3 *Bedrooms* | 2 *Full Baths* | 1 *Half Bath* |

PLAN #HPK3400136

Designed by Stephen Fuller, Inc.

First Floor: 1,780 sq. ft.

Second Floor: 1,216 sq. ft.

Total: 2,996 sq. ft.

Width: 50' – 4"

Depth: 43' – 0"

Foundation: Crawlspace

1-800-850-1491
eplans.com

First Floor

Second Floor

Shed with Style

PLAN #HPK3400085

Width: 8' – 0"

Depth: 10' – 0"

Height: 11' – 2"

1-800-850-1491
eplans.com

PERFECT ACCOMPANIMENT

Trimmed with rustic cedar shakes and featuring a metal roof, the shed is as charming as it is useful. During the day, skylights, windows, and a Dutch door let in natural light to illuminate the hardy and well-organized work spaces.

The main structure has a width of 8' – 0" and a depth of 10' – 0", plus a stoop measuring 3' – 6" deep. The area at the side of the shed covered by the roof extension is 6' – 3" by 10' – 0". Use this space to store weather-hardy equipment that doesn't need to be indoors.

Pegboards running floor to ceiling are a great way to let the space work flexibly. Use hooks and baskets for items that will get most use, such as tools. Upper areas of the pegboard setup should be reserved for lightweight shelving, to hold infrequently accessed items out of the way.

Simple counters are sturdy and have been placed at a comfortable height. Reserve storage beneath counters for heavier items, like potting soil and planters.

Before building any backyard structure, find out how local zoning laws deal with sheds and familiarize yourself with building codes. In some places, the building department is not concerned with sheds that are less than a certain square footage, and a permit will not be necessary. ❁

Dukes Folly

PLAN #HPK3400120

Width: 8' - 0"

Depth: 16' - 0"

Height: 16' - 0"

1-800-850-1491
eplans.com

PHOTOGRAPHY COURTESY OF SOUTHERN LIVING

Franklins Retreat

PLAN #HPK3400086

Width: 10' - 0"

Depth: 14' - 0"

Height: 16' - 0"

1-800-850-1491
eplans.com

PHOTOGRAPHY COURTESY OF SOUTHERN LIVING

Little Southern Charmer

ARCHITECTURAL RENDERING: STEPHEN FULLER, INC.

PLAN #HPK3400088

Width: 10' – 0"

Depth: 8' – 0"

Height: 10' – 0"

1-800-850-1491
eplans.com

Treehouse

PLAN #HPK3400089

Width: 18' – 0"

Depth: 14' – 0"

Height: 15' – 5" (variable)

1-800-850-1491
eplans.com

ARCHITECTURAL RENDERING: RAY WATKINS

196 square feet

Toolhouse

PLAN #HPK3400090

Width: 14' – 0"

Depth: 14' – 0"

Height: 12' – 0"

1-800-850-1491
eplans.com

100 square feet

Outdoor Retreat

PLAN #HPK3400091

Width: 10' – 0"

Depth: 10' – 0"

Height: 13' – 0"

1-800-850-1491
eplans.com

Storage Building

PLAN #HPK3400092

Width: 8' - 0"

Depth: 16' - 0"

Height: 12' - 0"

1-800-850-1491
eplans.com

PHOTOGRAPHY COURTESY OF SOUTHERN LIVING

Garden Getaway Shed

PLAN #HPK3400093

Width: 9' - 0"

Depth: 12' - 0"

Height: 16' - 0"

1-800-850-1491
eplans.com

PHOTOGRAPHY COURTESY OF SOUTHERN LIVING

Gothic Style Gazebo

PLAN #HPK3400094

Width: 12' - 0"

Depth: 12' - 0"

Height: 25' - 0"

1-800-850-1491
eplans.com

PHOTOGRAPHY COURTESY OF SOUTHERN LIVING

Garden Gazebo

PLAN #HPK3400096

Width: 15' - 0"

Depth: 15' - 0"

Height: 17' - 0"

1-800-850-1491
eplans.com

PHOTOGRAPHY COURTESY OF SOUTHERN LIVING

Pond House

288 square feet

PLAN #HPK3400097

Width: 12' – 0"

Depth: 24' – 0"

Height: 12' – 0"

1-800-850-1491
eplans.com

Playhouse

30 square feet

PLAN #HPK3400098

Width: 5' – 0"

Depth: 6' – 0"

Height: 12' – 0"

1-800-850-1491
eplans.com

Southern Living.
SELECTION, CONVENIENCE, SERVICE!

For 20 years, *Southern Living*® magazine has been collecting exclusive home plans from the South's top architects and designers. From formal and traditional homes, to casual and stylish vacation cottages, the *Southern Living* plan collection has been the favorite of the magazine's readers as well as other admirers of southern architecture.

The plans gathered here represent the very best of the Southern Living portfolio. Each home finds a unique balance of historically influenced exteriors—Neoclassical, Colonial, Craftsman, European—and modern approaches to interior layout. Along with beautifully presented formal spaces, each design caters to the comfort and convenience of homeowners with the inclusion of flexible utility spaces, such as mudrooms and offices. Outdoor living areas, present as extended entertaining spaces or as private retreats, are equally important features in the *Southern Living* home.

WHAT YOU'LL GET WITH YOUR ORDER

The contents of each designer's blueprint package is unique, but all contain detailed, high-quality working drawings. You can expect to find the following standard elements in most sets of plans:

ABOUT OUR PLANS

Southern Living working drawings offer a complete conceptual design of our homes. However, our working drawings do not include fully engineered construction documents.

Square Footage Estimates

The heated square footage estimate provided on the small-scale plan does not include the garage, porches, decks, bonus spaces, storage areas, or the basement level. We recommend that your builder verify all of the plan's dimensions and square footage calculations, taking into consideration any modifications or additions.

Also keep in mind that there are several different formulas for calculating square footage, and your builder's estimate may differ slightly from ours.

Estimating Construction Costs

Accurate construction-cost estimates should be made from the working drawings. We suggest consulting with a local builder to provide an estimate of those specific costs. Sometimes your builder can give you a ballpark estimate based on the information provided in the descriptions in this magazine. However, you will need working drawings for more accuracy.

After you order the plans, you may want to get at least two separate estimates from contractors for comparison because many variables can affect cost. The contractor should provide the material quantity lists; costs may vary depending on choice of materials, availability of materials within an area, labor costs, choice of finishes, and degree of detail.

Copy Restrictions and Copyright Information

All *Southern Living* House Plans are protected under the United States Copyright Law. Blueprints may not be resold, copied, or reproduced by any means. When you purchase a blueprint from *Southern Living* House Plans, you are licensed the right to build one residence. *Southern Living* designers and architects retain all rights, title, and ownership to the original design and documents.

What's Included in a Blueprint Package

*   **Foundations and floor-framing plans.** This shows the complete foundation layout, including drawings for a basement, slab, or crawlspace. Only one type is included with each plan. Support walls and all necessary dimensions are part of this sheet. Please note that there is no beam layout included with foundation plans.
*   **Dimensioned floor plans.** Each floor of the house is shown in detail. The position and dimensions of floors, windows, staircases, and columns are clearly indicated.
*   **Suggested electrical plans.** Included are suggestions for the placement of switches, outlets, and fixtures. Local code will dictate exact placement. This will be determined by your builder. Select plans may not include electrical plans.
*   **Typical wall section.** This cross section shows a typical wall from footings to roofline.
*   **Exterior elevations.** These pages provide drawings of the front, rear, left, and right sides of the house. They also suggest materials for the structure and detail work.
*   **Interior elevations.** This includes detailed drawings of cabinets, fireplaces, columns, other

built-in units, or suggested trim profiles. CHK Architects plans from the American Traditions Series do not include interior details.
*   **Suggested exterior and interior finish schedules.**
*   **Doors and window sizes.**

What's Not Included

*   **Heating and plumbing plans.** These plans should be supplied by local subcontractors.
*   **Material quantity lists.** Obtain these lists from the contractor you choose or from a local building materials supplier.
*   **Architectural and engineering seals.** Some cities and states require a licensed architect or engineer to review and seal, or officially approve, a blueprint prior to construction due to concerns over energy costs, safety, and other factors. Due to varying local requirements *Southern Living* House Plans is unable to offer these seals. Contact a local building official to find out if such a review is required.

Changing Your Plans

We encourage you to personalize your *Southern Living* House Plan. In an effort to make this process quicker and easier, we offer reproducible prints on all house plans. Please note that Reproducible files come with a one-time construction license and are not returnable.

Rear Elevations

If you would like to see a rear elevation, call toll-free 1-800-850-1491, or visit eplans.com. We offer a complimentary reduced sheet taken directly from our blueprints. This sheet cannot be used for construction purposes, but it will provide a detailed look at the back of the home.

Reverse Plans

Sometimes, to better site a house, it is necessary for the builder to use a reverse set of plans (often called a mirror image or flopped set). If your builder needs a reverse set, order one reverse and the rest standard sets of plans.

Building Codes

Our plans are designed to meet national building standards, but because of varying interpretations, and the fact that codes are subject to change, we cannot warrant compliance with any of the specific building codes and ordinances.

Your local builder or an engineer should review the plan you choose and ensure that it complies with all applicable building codes and subdivision restrictions. We are not responsible for any revisions or interpretations made by third parties involved in the construction of your homes.

BEFORE YOU CALL

You are making a terrific decision to use a pre-drawn house plan—it is one you can make with confidence, knowing that your blueprints are crafted by national-award-winning certified residential designers and architects, and trusted by builders.

Once you've selected the plan you want—or even if you have questions along the way—our experienced customer service representatives are available to help you navigate the home-building process. To help them provide you with even better service, please consider the following questions before you call:

■ **Have you chosen or purchased your lot?**
If so, please review the building setback requirements of your local building authority before you call. You don't need to have a lot before ordering plans, but if you own land already, please have the width and depth dimensions handy when you call.

■ **Have you chosen a builder?**
Involving your builder in the plan selection and evaluation process may be beneficial. Luckily, builders know they can have confidence with pre-drawn plans because they've been designed for livability, functionality, and typically are builder-proven at successful home sites across the country.

■ **Do you need a construction loan?**
Construction loans are unique because they involve determining the value of something that is not yet constructed. Several lenders offer convenient contstruction-to-permanent loans. It is important to choose a good lending partner—one who will help guide you through the application and appraisal process. Most will even help you evaluate your contractor to ensure reliability and credit worthiness.

■ **How many sets of plans do you need?**
Building a home can typically require a number of sets of blueprints—one for yourself, two or three for the builder and subcontractors, two for the local building department, and one or more for your lender. For this reason, we offer 8-, and Reproducible plan packages. Reproducible plans are tremendously flexible in that they allow you to make up to 12 duplicates of the plan so you have enough copies of the plan for everyone involved in the financing and construction of your home.

■ **Do you have to make any changes to meet local building codes?**
While all of our plans are drawn to meet national building codes at the time they were created, many areas required that plans be stamped by a local engineer to certify that they meet local building codes. Building codes are updated frequently and can vary by state, county, city, or municipality. Contact your local building inspection department, office of planning and zoning, or department of permits to determine how your local codes will affect your construction project. The best way to assure that you can make changes to your plan, if necessary, is to purchase a Reproducible Package.

■ **Has everyone—from family members to contractors—been involved in selecting the plan?**
Building a new home is an exciting process, and using pre-drawn plans is a great way to realize your dreams. Make sure that everyone involved has had an opportunity to review the plan you've selected. While Hanley Wood does have an exchange policy, it's best to be sure all parties agree on your selection before you buy.

CALL TOLL-FREE 1-800-850-1491

Source Key
HPK34

TERMS & CONDITIONS
OUR 90-DAY EXCHANGE POLICY

BUY WITH CONFIDENCE!

As *Southern Living*'s plan fulfillment partner, ePlans.com is committed to ensuring your satisfaction with your blueprint order, which is why we offer a 90-day exchange policy. With the exception of Reproducible Package orders, we will exchange your entire first order for an equal or greater number of blueprints from our plan collection within 90 days of the original order. The entire content of your original order must be returned before an exchange will be processed. Please call our customer service department at 1-888-690-1116 for your return authorization number and shipping instructions. If the returned blueprints look used, redlined, or copied, we will not honor your exchange. Fees for exchanging your blueprints are as follows: 20% of the amount of the original order, plus the difference in cost if exchanging for a design in a higher price bracket or less the difference in cost if exchanging for a design in a lower price bracket. (Because they can be copied, Reproducible blueprints are not exchangeable or refundable.) Please call for current postage and handling prices. Shipping and handling charges are not refundable.

ARCHITECTURAL AND ENGINEERING SEALS

Some cities and states now require that a licensed architect or engineer review and "seal" a blueprint, or officially approve it, prior to construction. Prior to application for a building permit or the start of actual construction, we strongly advise that you consult your local building official who can tell you if such a review is required.

LOCAL BUILDING CODES AND ZONING REQUIREMENTS

Each plan was designed to meet or exceed the requirements of a nationally recognized model building code in effect at the time and place the plan was drawn. Typically plans designed after the year 2000 conform to the International Residential Building Code (IRC 2000 or 2003). The IRC is comprised of portions of the three major codes below. Plans drawn before 2000 conform to one of the three recognized building codes in effect at the time: Building Officials and Code Administrators (BOCA)

International, Inc.; the Southern Building Code Congress International, (SBCCI) Inc.; the International Conference of Building Officials (ICBO); or the Council of American Building Officials (CABO).

Because of the great differences in geography and climate throughout the United States and Canada, each state, county, and municipality has its own building codes, zone requirements, ordinances, and building regulations. Your plan may need to be modified to comply with local requirements. In addition, you may need to obtain permits or inspections from local governments before and in the course of construction. We authorize the use of the blueprints on the express condition that you consult a local licensed architect or engineer of your choice prior to beginning construction and strictly comply with all local building codes, zoning requirements, and other applicable laws, regulations, ordinances, and requirements. Notice: Plans for homes to be built in Nevada must be redrawn by a Nevada-registered professional. Consult your local building official for more information on this subject.

TERMS AND CONDITIONS

These designs are protected under the terms of United States Copyright Law and may not be copied or reproduced in any way, by any means, unless you have purchased a Reproducible Plan Package and signed the

accompanying license to modify and copy the plan, which clearly indicates your right to modify, copy, or reproduce. We authorize the use of your chosen design as an aid in the construction of ONE (1) single- or multifamily home only. You may not use this design to build a second dwelling or multiple dwellings without purchasing another blueprint or blueprints or paying additional design fees. Multi-use fees vary by designer—please call one of our experienced sales representatives for a quote.

DISCLAIMER

The designers we work with have put substantial care and effort into the creation of their blueprints. However, because we cannot provide on-site consultation, supervision, and control over actual construction, and because of the great variance in local building requirements, building practices, and soil, seismic, weather, and other conditions, WE MAKE NO WARRANTY OF ANY KIND, EXPRESS OR IMPLIED, WITH RESPECT TO THE CONTENT OR USE OF THE BLUEPRINTS, INCLUDING BUT NOT LIMITED TO ANY WARRANTY OF MERCHANTABILITY OR OF FITNESS FOR A PARTICULAR PURPOSE. ITEMS, PRICES, TERMS, AND CONDITIONS ARE SUBJECT TO CHANGE WITHOUT NOTICE.

**CALL TOLL FREE
1-800-850-1491
OR VISIT
EPLANS.COM**

IMPORTANT COPYRIGHT NOTICE

From the Council of Publishing Home Designers

Blueprints for residential construction (or working drawings, as they are often called in the industry) are copyrighted intellectual property, protected under the terms of the United States Copyright Law and, therefore, cannot be copied legally for use in building. The following are some guidelines to help you get what you need to build your home, without violating copyright law:

1. HOME PLANS ARE COPYRIGHTED

Just like books, movies, and songs, home plans receive protection under the federal copyright laws. The copyright laws prevent anyone, other than the copyright owner, from reproducing, modifying, or reusing the plans or design without permission of the copyright owner.

2. DO NOT COPY DESIGNS OR FLOOR PLANS FROM ANY PUBLICATION, ELECTRONIC MEDIA, OR EXISTING HOME

It is illegal to copy, change, or redraw home designs found in a plan book, CDROM or on the Internet. The right to modify plans is one of the exclusive rights of copyright. It is also illegal to copy or redraw a constructed home that is protected by copyright, even if you have never seen the plans for the home. If you find a plan or home that you like, you must purchase a set of plans from an authorized source. The plans may not be lent, given away, or sold by the purchaser.

3. DO NOT USE PLANS TO BUILD MORE THAN ONE HOUSE

The original purchaser of house plans is typically licensed to build a single home from the plans. Building more than one home from the plans without permission is an infringement of the home designer's copyright. The purchase of a multiple-set package of plans is for the construction of a single home only. The purchase of additional sets of plans does not grant the right to construct more than one home.

4. HOUSE PLANS IN THE FORM OF BLUEPRINTS OR BLACKLINES CANNOT BE COPIED OR REPRODUCED

Plans, blueprints, or blacklines, unless they are reproducibles, cannot be copied or reproduced without prior written consent of the copyright owner. Copy shops and blueprinters are prohibited from making copies of these plans without the copyright release letter you receive with reproducible plans.

5. HOUSE PLANS IN THE FORM OF BLUEPRINTS OR BLACKLINES CANNOT BE REDRAWN

Plans cannot be modified or redrawn without first obtaining the copyright owner's permission. With your purchase of plans, you are licensed to make non-structural changes by "red-lining" the purchased plans. If you need to make structural changes or need to redraw the plans for any reason, you must purchase a reproducible set of plans (see topic 6) which includes a license to modify the plans. Blueprints do not come with a license to make structural changes or to redraw the plans. You may not reuse or sell the modified design.

6. REPRODUCIBILE HOME PLANS

Reproducible plans (for example sepias, mylars, CAD files, electronic files, and vellums) come with a license to make modifications to the plans. Once modified, the plans can be taken to a local copy shop or blueprinter to make up to 10 or 12 copies of the plans to use in the construction of a single home. Only one home can be constructed from any single purchased set of reproducible plans either in original form or as modified. The license to modify and copy must be completed and returned before the plan will be shipped.

7. MODIFIED DESIGNS CANNOT BE REUSED

Even if you are licensed to make modifications to a copyrighted design, the modified design is not free from the original designer's copyright. The sale or reuse of the modified design is prohibited. Also, be aware that any modification to plans relieves the original designer from liability for design defects and voids all warranties expressed or implied.

8. WHO IS RESPONSIBLE FOR COPYRIGHT INFRINGEMENT?

Any party who participates in a copyright violation may be responsible including the purchaser, designers, architects, engineers, drafters, homeowners, builders, contractors, sub-contractors, copy shops, blueprinters, developers, and real estate agencies. It does not matter whether or not the individual knows that a violation is being committed. Ignorance of the law is not a valid defense.

9. PLEASE RESPECT HOME DESIGN COPYRIGHTS

In the event of any suspected violation of a copyright, or if there is any uncertainty about the plans purchased, the publisher, architect, designer, or the Council of Publishing Home Designers (www.cphd.org) should be contacted before proceeding. Awards are some-times offered for information about home design copyright infringement.

10. PENALTIES FOR INFRINGEMENT

Penalties for violating a copyright may be severe. The responsible parties are required to pay actual damages caused by the infringement (which may be substantial), plus any profits made by the infringer's commissions to include all profits from the sale of any home built from an infringing design. The copyright law also allows for the recovery of statutory damages, which may be as high as $150,000 for each infringement. Finally, the infringer may be required to pay legal fees which often exceed the damages.

PAGE	PLAN #	PLAN NAME	1-SET PACKAGE	8-SET PACKAGE	REPRODUCIBLE PACKAGE
34	HPK3400031	Oak Creek	N/A	$575	$795
35	HPK3400041	Beachside Bungalow	N/A	$575	$795
36	HPK3400012	Hilltop	N/A	$575	$795
37	HPK3400033	Crooked Creek	N/A	$575	$795
38	HPK3400032	Eagle's Nest	N/A	$685	$955
39	HPK3400027	Smokey Creek	N/A	$575	$795
40	HPK3400014	Little Red	N/A	$685	$955
41	HPK3400019	Grayson Trail	N/A	$685	$955
42	HPK3400034	Mill Springs	N/A	$685	$955
44	HPK3400013	Deer Run	N/A	$685	$955
45	HPK3400028	The Ozarks	N/A	$685	$955
46	HPK3400017	Walnut Cove	N/A	$865	$1,195
47	HPK3400081	Foxglove Cottage	N/A	$685	$955
48	HPK3400020	Fox River	N/A	$865	$1,195
49	HPK3400018	Hunting Creek Alternate	N/A	$765	$1,065
50	HPK3400080	Chestnut Lane	N/A	$685	$955
51	HPK3400029	Dogtrot	N/A	$685	$955
52	HPK3400030	Sweetwater	N/A	$685	$955
53	HPK3400008	Banning Court	N/A	$865	$1,195
54	HPK3400119	Nautical Cottage	$225	$985	$1,365
55	HPK3400075	Caribbean Getaway	N/A	$685	$955
56	HPK3400050	Rustic Beach Cottage	N/A	$765	$1,065
57	HPK3400115	Spinnerbait Retreat	$225	$765	$1,065
58	HPK3400060	Heather Place	N/A	$765	$1,065
59	HPK3400035	River Birch	N/A	$765	$1,065
60	HPK3400078	Forsythia	N/A	$765	$1,065
61	HPK3400079	Gardenia	N/A	$685	$955
62	HPK3400016	Hunting Creek	N/A	$765	$1,065
63	HPK3400009	Ashley River Cottage	N/A	$765	$1,065
64	HPK3400036	Ellsworth Cottage	N/A	$765	$1,065
65	HPK3400062	Sage House	N/A	$865	$1,195
66	HPK3400111	Stripers Cottage	$225	$765	$1,065
68	HPK3400056	Coosaw River Cottage	N/A	$985	$1,365
69	HPK3400063	Tidewater Retreat	N/A	$985	$1,365
70	HPK3400010	Ashton	N/A	$865	$1,195
71	HPK3400043	Beaufort Cottage	N/A	$865	$1,195
72	HPK3400129	Silverhill	N/A	$865	$1,195
73	HPK3400021	Bucksport Cottage	N/A	$765	$1,065
74	HPK3400108	Topwater Lodge	$225	$765	$1,065
76	HPK3400061	Wisteria	N/A	$985	$1,365
77	HPK3400083	Capeside Cottage	N/A	$865	$1,195
78	HPK3400104	Skitter Creek Cottage	$225	$765	$1,065
79	HPK3400105	Shad Shack Retreat	$225	$765	$1,065
80	HPK3400024	Gresham Creek Cottage	N/A	$765	$1,065
81	HPK3400126	Jasmine	N/A	$765	$1,065
82	HPK3400113	Fly-Ty Retreat	$225	$865	$1,195
84	HPK3400046	Piedmont Cottage	N/A	$985	$1,365
85	HPK3400070	Turtle Lake Cottage	N/A	$865	$1,195
86	HPK3400122	Winonna Park	N/A	$865	$1,195
87	HPK3400058	River Cliff Cottage	N/A	$1,375	$1,905
88	HPK3400100	Twitchin Minnow	$225	$765	$1,065
90	HPK3400101	Lil Popper	$225	$765	$1,065
91	HPK3400057	Windsong Cottage	N/A	$685	$955
92	HPK3400022	Elizabeths Place	N/A	$765	$1,065
93	HPK3400106	Bucketmouth Bungalow	$225	$865	$1,195
94	HPK3400107	Cricket Cottage	$225	$865	$1,195
95	HPK3400048	Bermuda Bluff Cottage	N/A	$1,125	$1,555
96	HPK3400112	Specks River Cottage	$225	$765	$1,065
98	HPK3400116	Whitefish Retreat	$225	$985	$1,365
99	HPK3400064	Spartina Cottage	N/A	$865	$1,195
100	HPK3400071	Walterboro Ridge	N/A	$765	$1,065
101	HPK3400123	West Bay Landing	N/A	$1,595	$2,205
102	HPK3400040	Barrier Island Escape	N/A	$865	$1,195
103	HPK3400068	Ogletree Lane	N/A	$765	$1,065
104	HPK3400025	Cotton Hill Cottage	N/A	$765	$1,065
105	HPK3400042	Couples Cottage	N/A	$865	$1,195
106	HPK3400124	Chinaberry	N/A	$765	$1,065

PAGE	PLAN #	PLAN NAME	1-SET PACKAGE	8-SET PACKAGE	REPRODUCIBLE PACKAGE
107	HPK3400023	Williams Bluff	N/A	$765	$1,065
108	HPK3400005	Lowcountry Cottage	N/A	$865	$1,195
109	HPK3400026	Maple Hill	N/A	$765	$1,065
110	HPK3400049	Inlet Retreat	N/A	$985	$1,365
111	HPK3400072	Summer Cottage	N/A	$765	$1,065
112	HPK3400067	Carlisle House	N/A	$765	$1,065
113	HPK3400006	Aiken Ridge	N/A	$985	$1,365
114	HPK3400038	New Rustic Oaks	N/A	$865	$1,195
115	HPK3400007	Bradley House	N/A	$985	$1,365
116	HPK3400102	Mad Trapper	$225	$865	$1,195
117	HPK3400103	Spincaster Cottage	$225	$865	$1,195
118	HPK3400117	Harborside Hideaway	$225	$865	$1,195
120	HPK3400069	Angel Oak Point	N/A	$765	$1,065
121	HPK3400047	River View Cottage	N/A	$985	$1,365
122	HPK3400065	Wildmere Cottage	N/A	$685	$955
123	HPK3400125	Franklin House	N/A	$1,375	$1,905
124	HPK3400131	Winnsboro Heights	N/A	$765	$1,065
125	HPK3400132	Tabor Lane	N/A	$765	$1,065
126	HPK3400128	Rambert Place	N/A	$765	$1,065
127	HPK3400118	2007 Cottage Living Idea Home	$225	$985	$1,365
128	HPK3400082	Mabry Cottage	N/A	$865	$1,195
129	HPK3400054	Peachtree Cottage	N/A	$865	$1,195
130	HPK3400001	Lakeside Cottage	N/A	$1,595	$2,205
131	HPK3400127	Pennington Point	N/A	$865	$1,195
132	HPK3400002	New Oxford	N/A	$1,125	$1,555
133	HPK3400044	Glenview Cottage	N/A	$865	$1,195
134	HPK3400099	Downing Cottage	$225	$985	$1,365
135	HPK3400076	Pleasant Hill Cottage	N/A	$865	$1,195
136	HPK3400004	Westbury Park	N/A	$985	$1,365
137	HPK3400130	St. Helena House	N/A	$865	$1,195
138	HPK3400015	Stonebridge Cottage	N/A	$985	$1,365
139	HPK3400045	Our Gulf Coast Cottage	N/A	$985	$1,365
140	HPK3400011	Cottage Of The Year	N/A	$1,595	$2,205
141	HPK3400133	Camden Cottage	N/A	$1,375	$1,905
142	HPK3400077	Pine Hill Cottage	N/A	$865	$1,195
143	HPK3400134	Bluff Haven	N/A	$765	$1,065
144	HPK3400084	Family Central	N/A	$765	$1,065
145	HPK3400053	Poplar Creek Cottage	N/A	$865	$1,195
146	HPK3400052	Spring Lake Cottage	N/A	$1,375	$1,905
147	HPK3400059	Alta Vista	N/A	$1,375	$1,905
148	HPK3400066	Turnball Park	N/A	$985	$1,365
149	HPK3400039	Elderberry Place	N/A	$865	$1,195
150	HPK3400135	Grissom Trail	N/A	$765	$1,065
151	HPK3400109	Bucktail Lodge	$225	$985	$1,365
152	HPK3400110	Rattling Shad	$225	$985	$1,365
153	HPK3400073	Harborside Cottage	N/A	$765	$1,065
154	HPK3400114	Hookset Hideaway	$225	$865	$1,195
156	HPK3400051	Sea Island House	N/A	$2,375	$3,285
157	HPK3400003	McKenzie Cottage	N/A	$765	$1,065
158	HPK3400037	Bay Point Cottage	N/A	$865	$1,195
159	HPK3400074	Bedford Cottage	N/A	$985	$1,365
160	HPK3400121	Hampstead Place	$225	$1,125	$1,555
161	HPK3400136	Blount Springs	N/A	$1,375	$1,905
162	HPK3400085	Shed With Style	$40	N/A	N/A
164	HPK3400120	Dukes Folly	$40	N/A	N/A
164	HPK3400086	Franklins Retreat	$40	N/A	N/A
165	HPK3400088	Little Southern Charmer	$60	N/A	N/A
165	HPK3400089	Treehouse	$40	N/A	N/A
166	HPK3400090	Toolhouse	$40	N/A	N/A
166	HPK3400091	Outdoor Retreat	$40	N/A	N/A
167	HPK3400092	Storage Building	$40	N/A	N/A
167	HPK3400093	Garden Getaway Shed	$40	N/A	N/A
168	HPK3400094	Gothic Style Gazebo	$40	N/A	N/A
168	HPK3400096	Garden Gazebo	$40	N/A	N/A
169	HPK3400097	Pond House	$40	N/A	N/A
169	HPK3400098	Playhouse	$40	N/A	N/A

ORDER BLUEPRINTS ANYTIME AT EPLANS.COM OR 1-800-850-1491